Six Dogs

A Sled

And Me!

Ken Robertshaw

Copyright © Ken Robertshaw
ISBN: 9781520146096

With love to my wife Pauline for letting me pursue my dreams while staying behind and worrying.

To Kenneth and Rebecca for being my friends and for Helen (and bump) and Paul for making them complete

For my personal trainer Bess – sorry you couldn't come.

Special thanks are due to Pat Lloyd for her patience in editing this work

Dedicated to the memory of Graham Whalley for starting it all in the first place.

Foreword

André Poulie, Co-founder and President of The Theodora Children's trust

One should never doubt the power of a child's dream. There was Ken, 8 years old, daydreaming of the adventures of his "uncle" Graham in the Arctic regions. Ken's adventure is the living proof that a child's dream is an amazing treasure. It becomes deeply imbedded in an adult's heart and acts a beacon of hope in life's darkest moments. It is there to remind us that life is precious and that we need to stop just for a second to think about it. Having embarked on an incredible challenge, Ken writes that the simple things in life really are the best. They can be found just in the form of a cup of tea.

Health is one of our biggest treasures and this becomes a self-evident truth when one has to fight to regain it. Breathing, walking, moving your arms, creating things with your hands and soul, thinking, loving and sharing, all these are our treasures; they are the gifts of life.

Ken has known enormous challenges, particularly when his knee had to be replaced. Regaining his mobility was the order of the day and he would spend many hours each day in physiotherapy. Never for a second would he have believed at that moment that he would lead a team of huskies for 250 kilometres across the frozen wilderness of the Arctic in temperatures of minus 25 degrees.

This reminds me of my own experience as a child, when a serious accident left my right food severely damaged. The accident taught me discipline as without it, it would have been impossible to walk again. It also gave me a never-ending sense of appreciation for the support of the hospital staff. They were there every little step of the way, until that unforgettable journey when I could walk with my own feet out of hospital and breathe fresh air again.

During my unending hospital months, a tree proudly standing next to my hospital window became my imaginary world. My mother, Theodora, came to my bedside every day, her arms full of games and books to make my imagination wonder outside of the white hospital walls. Theodora was the captain of my ship and her tales, a life line to hold on to. She was all generosity and courage even when she embraced a daunting fight and a dance with cancer. She did not make it through but her humour lives on.

It is a great honour to be part of the Theodora Children's Trust team as we meet wonderful and generous souls like Ken. To our Rotary club friends, to all of you who helped Ken realize his childhood dream, we send our gratitude. The same is true for you, dear reader, as in purchasing this book you gave life to a smile on a child's face, somewhere in a UK hospital. Let it shine as a beacon.

To Ken, I express our friendship and admiration for what he did surely represents something extraordinary. In reading this book, you will share in the spirit of adventure and who knows… a child's dream is never far away.

André Poulie

Table of contents

Halifax, West Yorkshire, England – N 53⁰ 41'632 W 1⁰ 51'329
  3

Halifax to Heathrow Airport, England – N 51⁰ 28'789 W 0⁰ 27'015
  9

Heathrow Airport, England to Tromso, Norway – N 69⁰ 38'921 E18⁰ 57'444
  11

Singnaldalen, Tromso, to 1st Camp – N 69° 4'465 E 20° 8'515
  14

1st camp to 2nd camp – N 68° 57'842 E 20° 21'182
  19

2nd camp to 3rd camp – N 68° 44'260 N 20° 22'475 E
  26

3rd camp to 4th camp – N 68° 22'076 E 20° 02'557
  34

Photographs
  40

4th camp to 5th camp – N 68° 00'537 E 20° 23'626
  45

5th camp to Kiruna, Sweden – N 67° 50'893 E 20° 33'804
  51

Tromso, Norway to Heathrow airport, England
  58

Appendix i – The Theodora Children's Trust
  59

Appendix ii – Sponsors
  60

Appendix iii – Equipment
  61

Appendix iv – Physiological and Psychological effects
  62

25th September 2011 – 23rd March 2012
Halifax, West Yorkshire
N 53⁰ 41'632 W 1⁰ 51'329

When I was about 8, a friend of the family, who in good Northern Tradition, was known as "uncle" Graham, went away to work in the Arctic regions of Alaska. I never really knew what he did but seem to remember that it was something to do with runways for airplanes.

Whatever it was he always had tales to tell about the extremely low temperatures, huge amounts of snow and the difficulties of living and working in that environment. About how vehicle engines had to be kept running or they would freeze solid, about the man who gripped a lorry door handle without gloves on and permanently damaged his hand.

What small boy wouldn't be enthralled by tales from a world so different from the one he lived in?

And so began a lifelong fascination with Polar exploration. I would visit the library to read books on Scott, Shackleton and Amundsen and pore over photos of the regions. I was fascinated and enthralled by the sheer hard work of staying alive, never mind actually climbing mountains or surviving the ice floes breaking up under them as they crossed the frozen seas. The early part of the 20th Century was known as the heroic age of Polar exploration and for good reason. These men would set off to the southern polar region without actually knowing what they would face, there were no maps or even oral history of the region and that most valuable of tools we use today, satellite images, hadn't even been thought of. There was not even long distance communication as radio was still in its infancy.

The North Pole offered no less of a challenge than its southern sibling although the high northern latitudes of Europe and the North American region had actually had inhabitants for longer than recorded history in the shape of the Sámi and Inuit people. They only inhabited the land mass areas whereas the northern Polar Cap actually covers an area of the Arctic Ocean. The actual pole may well be permanently frozen but the surrounding areas are subject to forces of tide, wind and temperature that causes them to shift making mapping and recording them impossible.

All of this, along with tales of the expeditions to find the North West Passage that would open up the trading routes across northern Canada left their mark on me.

Like most lads in the 1960's I was in the Boys Brigade, until the company folded, and the Scouts, until I discovered girls, and enjoyed the weekend camps and summer holiday trips which introduced us "Townies" to the countryside and so began another love of mine, walking.

Over the years it has become something of a cliché to refer to any northern town, especially those in the industrial West Riding of Yorkshire, as being grim and grimy and Halifax, where I grew up, was no exception. Let me tell you that it is a well-earned epithet. The smoke from the mill chimneys and coal fires in just about every house had left the walls of buildings blackened with air pollution, the air was permanently awash with fine dust that seemed to settle on everything and there were always different smells pervading the atmosphere dependent on which way the wind was blowing and which factory was in full production. The only good news was when Rowntree Mackintosh vented steam from their boilers and the town smelled of chocolate. A bit like I imagine the town featured in Roald Dahl's 'Willie Wonka and the chocolate factory' only without the Oompa Loompas running around the place. So the opportunity to get away from it all was a gift not to be missed.

Halifax is fortunate in this respect as it is situated right on the edge of the Pennine range and within easy travelling distance of the Yorkshire dales. A walk in the countryside was never far away and once in and around the surrounding hills the rolling green vistas were a tonic not to be missed. It is something I cherish to this day and still enjoy walking familiar routes that have the ability to take one away from the daily grind. It might not cure all ills but it certainly helps to lift the spirits.

An unremarkable school career occupied my teenage years, being the first member of the family to go to grammar school made my mother and grandparents happy as they, like every generation before, wanted a better life for their children and saw education as a way of achieving it. That and good old-fashioned hard work. I say unremarkable, as I never did live up to the academic expectations of the school, although I remember some of the teachers with great fondness as they tried to encourage me. The ones that had more direct or forceful methods are best consigned to the dustbin of memory. I am not proud of the fact that I never obtained a qualification in mathematics or that my grades were not exactly stellar but I am grateful for the opportunity that was offered to me. I went on to obtain all manner of degrees and diplomas as I, like many, found the thrill of learning late in life and applied myself to the discipline needed. I always tell young people I work with that the beginning of life is the time to acquire qualifications but there is never a time to stop learning.

After leaving school I joined the, then, West Yorkshire Constabulary, a career I followed for the next 28 years, eventually retiring at the rank of Inspector. Somebody once said to me that Police Middle Management is full of failed Grammar School boys and you can take it from me that it's true! Along the way I gained a hatful of qualifications and a lot of experience in driving, computer skills, administration, personnel management, decision-making and firearms use. Fortunately I have not had to employ that last skill but I still know which end to hold and which end to point.

In 1979, six years into my career, I sustained an injury to my left knee, when I attended the report of a man breaking into a cottage out in the rural part of town.

Together with a colleague I attended and as he went to the front of the building I went to the back, arriving just as 'Billy Burglar' decided to try and escape by jumping out of the upstairs window.

Unfortunately, for me that is, he fell on top of me as I rounded the corner of the building. In breaking his fall I twisted, as my legs gave way, and his head landed on my knee protecting him from injury. My colleague came to my aid and he was carted off to the cells whilst I was taken to hospital.

The ensuing injury required surgery to repair and took me off my feet for quite some time. It is also unfortunate that this did not fully cure the problem as I had another two operations to trim the cartilage in the following years. This probably would have been the end of it all had I not been knocked down by a car whilst crossing the road in 1996! This time I was on a day out with some children who were being given a 'treat' by The Rotary Club of Halifax and I was crossing over to buy some extra chocolate bars for them. Sorry, I forgot to mention that the car was travelling the wrong way down a one-way street and by now I held the rank of Inspector in the Police. I wish I could have seen the drivers' face but I was on my way to hospital. Again.

Over the years another two routine 'trimmings' followed until, in 2005, the condition of my leg had deteriorated so much that I had half of my left knee replaced with a prosthetic insert. That was the 6th operation on my leg and whilst not as bad as some people have to endure, was not exactly a barrel of laughs. Hospitals are not renowned for being fun palaces despite the care and attention offered by every member of the staff in them.

One thing my career in the Police Service did lead to was involvement in a charity group, which took relief goods to orphanages in Romania following the collapse of the communist regime in 1990. The goods were transported in convoys of lorries and I was asked to help as I have a Heavy Goods Vehicle driving licence.

Trucking medical and other much-needed equipment across Europe introduced me to a whole new world of need.

As part of the process I was invited to speak to various groups about my experience in return for cash donations for the cause. One of these groups was the Rotary Club of Halifax in May of 1992. By now I was posted to Halifax as the Station Inspector and was in my element, organising Policing for my hometown. The talk to the Rotary Club led them to invite me to join them, an invitation I accepted and have never regretted since, as I have met some wonderful people, been involved in numerous cultural exchanges and been able to make a difference in peoples' lives.

In 2007 I was elected as the District Governor for Rotary in East, North and West Yorkshire by the constituent clubs and took on responsibility for the leadership of the District. One part of this role is to host the annual conference at which club members have the opportunity to learn about new projects, get an update on existing ones and hear about schemes that are under consideration. There is also a great fellowship side to it so don't think it is all one big bore!

About a year before the conference I had been visiting a club located near to the South Yorkshire border. The speaker that night was from The Sheffield Children's Hospital who informed us of the many technical advances that were being made in that branch of medicine. She also mentioned, almost in passing, that they were trying to introduce a charity into the hospital that provided what she described as 'Clown Doctors' to help with the recuperation of the children. Intrigued by this, I did some research when back at home and found that she was referring to The Theodora Children's Trust, a charity aimed solely at providing entertainment to terminally and seriously ill children during their stay in hospital, working on the principle that laughter is the best medicine.

After some further research and discussions with Sarika Brown, the Executive director of the charity, I invited them to be our entertainment/speakers at the Saturday lunch event of the conference. What an event it turned out to be! We deliberately didn't tell the conference delegates what was happening so you can imagine their surprise when two young women dressed in white doctors coats', decorated with brightly coloured cartoon like characters and with faces painted up like circus clowns, began to circulate and make balloon animals, perform magic tricks or merely stick red foam noses on people at random. It was chaos and I loved it.

At the end of lunch Sarika gave a short address about the foundation and aims of the charity and I presented them with a cheque for £500 this being the surplus from the luncheon expenses. All I ever intended was the introduction of what I thought was a fantastic charity that did so much for young people in hospital, little did I think that the clubs in the district would take the charity to their hearts and over the next year donated almost £8000. This in turn led the Trust to start visiting the Children's ward of the Bradford Royal Infirmary and making life that bit more bearable for families in our area.

The connection between the Theodora Trust and myself continued and at the request of various clubs I have been pleased to act as a speaker for the charity, and to accept further donations on their behalf and to meet the joint founder of the charity, Andre Poulie, on several occasions, the most notable being at the café in Bradford Royal Infirmary where the Giggle Doctor (their official name) caused mirth, merriment and few strange looks while we tried to be serious. She won, we gave up.

In September of 2011 I received an email from Sarika with containing a link to a website, and the simple one line message 'Have a look at this and see if you want to have a go'. Intrigued, I opened the link to find that it was an invitation to take part in a Husky Challenge in March of 2012, where a group of up to 20 people would be travelling from Tromso in Norway to Kiruna in Sweden by dog sled team. The route was 350 kilometres above the Arctic Circle and participants would travel the 250 kilometres of its length in six days, driving their own sled teams, camping, cooking all their own food and attending to the dogs. The whole nine yards!

As you can imagine it took about as long to decide as it did to read the first line. A chance to fulfil a life's ambition and raise money for a favourite charity, count me in! It wasn't until about an hour later that I thought I had better tell Pauline, my wife, of my plans. She thought I was mad then and still does.

The challenge was organised by a company called Global Adventure Challenges and it was just one of a series that they offer including the usual Great Wall of China and Kilimanjaro treks. The cost of the program is just over £2000 and they offer two ways to pay. The first is commit to raising £3500 and make all donations through them; they take out their costs and pass the balance to your nominated charity. They also operate a direct giving site that collects on line donations on your behalf and then, for a fee, passes them on to the charity. The second way is to pay for the challenge direct and then collect donations for the charity separately. I elected to follow the second path given that I had access to fund raising through my membership of Rotary and I did not want to see a commercial organisation take a cut from my efforts.

I set myself an initial target of £5000 but had passed this by the beginning of December 2011 so revised it. I found that this revision would need to be carried out at least twice as I met and passed my targets.

One of the conditions made by the organisers was a medical report given that I have the prosthetic knee, so off to the doctor I went. He listened to what I was proposing to do and declared that in his opinion I was fit enough to take part. He then told me he thought that I was mad. Had Pauline been colluding with him?

So, fully signed up, fees paid and information pack received, I was ready for the next
Stage – increasing my fitness levels. Fortunately there is a Tennis and Squash Club located about 250 yards away from my home. It has a well-equipped gym and a pair of resident trainers who are able to work out programmes that are suited to the client's age, physical condition and needs. Not ever having been one for gym membership on the grounds that only fit people go to them, I approached this setup with no small amount of trepidation. My fears were instantly allayed when I discussed my requirements with Martin, the trainer on duty that day. He assured me that I was far from the most out of shape person ever to walk in and want to get fit and that it was all a case of start at a low level and build up over a number of weeks and months.

He worked out a program that would benefit my overall stamina and upper body strength and at the beginning of October 2011 I started on my three times a week routine. I had always thought that I had a reasonable level of fitness, as a result of walking my dog, Bess, twice a day and generally keeping on the move, but soon learned that it could be improved upon. From a small set of repetitions on various machines and sessions on static bikes and rowing machines, I gradually built up my physical condition. In the process I lost just over 6 kilos in weight and trimmed a bit off the 'spare tyre' I was carrying around. This was kept up until the week before I left for the expedition when I had only two light training sessions and loaded my meals with carbohydrate to build my energy reserves for the trip.

The organising company, Global Adventure Challenges, had provided me with a list of equipment that I would need to take as well as advising on what equipment would be provided. This, coupled with my readings on polar exploration, gave me a better than fair idea of what to expect. They also advised me that a member of the company staff would be accompanying us and that we would have an opportunity to meet him on the 4th of March, twenty days before we set off. I jumped at the chance and travelled to Cannock Chase, Staffordshire for the meeting, where I met Mike Hammond, the company representative

It turned out that Mike is involved in Husky racing in the UK, where they use sleds with wheels to overcome the lack of snow, and that he was not actually a paid member of the 'Global' staff. The company paid for his travel, equipment and food and he used his holidays from work to afford the time. Not a bad arrangement I suppose, he gets more experience as a sled rider and they get someone on the ground without the need of employing a specialist for the three times a year they run the event.

Mikes' advice was very practical and delivered with a sense of humour that both highlighted and played down the problems we would face. He was also able to give us our first look at the equipment we would be issued with and this enabled me to plan a little better for the kit I would need to source and take with me. I got on well with him from our first meeting, he is ex military, which gave us something of a common mind-set, and I was delighted to hear that he would be on the team that I was travelling with.

Those last twenty days saw me laying out gear on the spare bed, checking it, swapping it, adding to it, taking away from it and throwing it all in a pile and starting again, more times than I am sure I care to remember. One thing I did make sure of was that I had batteries aplenty for the various cameras and other electrical devices; several packs of chocolate bars and other snacks, an insulated mug and two flasks. As is the norm with packing for a trip I had more spare clothing than I actually needed; how much more would become apparent later but suffice it to say that most of it never saw the outside of my bag never mind the outside world.

As part of my personal preparation I gave up shaving as of the 1st of February. I also gave up cutting my hair but as I have nothing on top I doubted anyone would notice, and by the time came to set off I had a full beard that, sadly, was mostly white, making me look like some sort of bald Father Christmas. I at least looked like a Polar explorer even if I never had been.

In the last few days it was also possible to 'meet' some of my fellow adventurers through Facebook as the company had set up a page for us all to contact each other. It was only marginally useful as how well can you get to know someone through a short typed message? Still at least I had photos, which was a start. It turned out that the bulk of the group came from the Isle of Man and that they were raising funds for the Island's Children's Home. There were three other team members who live in the London area, two of them being a couple, or 'partners' in modern speak.

Planning packing and training over it was time for the first stage of the journey, and the one that was probably most stressful, the trip from home to Heathrow airport! If I have asked myself once I must have asked a thousand times, why did we have to use Heathrow? With the majority of us being from the north and Manchester offering flights with Scandinavian Airline Services (SAS) to Norway twice a day, it would have made more sense for us to use that airport. Obviously this didn't occur to the company so we had to add an extra day, and expense, to the trip by travelling down the night before and staying in a hotel.

Friday 23rd March 2012
Halifax to Heathrow airport
N 51⁰ 28'789 W 0⁰ 27'015

Sarika, from the Theodora Children's Trust, had called a couple of days before departure to say that she would be in the area of Heathrow on the Friday afternoon and would it be possible to meet up. I had already decided that I would leave after the morning rush hour had died down so that I didn't get caught up in the afternoon jams down south, when everyone would be trying to get away from the city for the weekend, so meeting her would not be a problem. Surprisingly the traffic was light all the way down and other than a couple of phone calls I had a restful journey.

One of the phone calls was from Mike Hammond, which surprised me somewhat. He told me that since our last meeting he had had a small operation on his left leg to correct something that occurred as a result of him breaking his leg on a Dog Sled Trip the previous year. I find it comforting that an experienced sled driver can break a leg when the organisers proudly tell us all that none of the paying participants had suffered any serious injuries. The result of this was that he would not be able to travel on the sleds with us but would still travel with us to set us off and bring us home.

He asked what level of first aid qualification I had and when I told him that I was a current 'first aid at work' certificate holder he said "Great, you can take the company first aid kit in your sled with you" then cheerily said "Goodbye, see you at the airport and we can talk at length later".

As I was pulling into the car park of the hotel I realised that I couldn't remember putting my hiking boots in to the car. A check in the boot as soon as I stopped brought my fears to life, I hadn't brought them. It had not been clear whether we were being provided with special cold weather boots, or just waterproof over-boots for wearing on the sled; in any event a sturdy pair would be needed just for walking about around camp and in Tromso. This would mean a trip into town, wherever that might be, to buy some new ones.

The hotel staff were tremendously helpful. They searched the internet for the nearest outdoor clothing shop, got me the address, printed off a map and even rang to check what time the shop would closed so that I could be sure of getting some boots.

I had my meeting with Sarika, which I had to cut short, to make a dash into the nearest town. After what must be the fastest boot fitting and purchase in history I returned to the hotel. By now, of course, the traffic was horrible, so far from missing the rush hour I was stuck in it. But at least I had boots!

It was whilst sitting in a traffic jam on the motorway back to the hotel, that I had a text message from my daughter in law Helen, who is expecting her first baby, and my first grandchild, in early August. This had provided much mirth for the family as I constantly complained that I was not old enough to be a grandparent and steadfastly refused to be called 'Granddad'. Of course they all did it every time they saw me. Helen had been for her first ultrasound scan and had sent me a copy of the photo attached to the text.

As I sat surrounded by a sea of strangers all going nowhere fast I realised that this image would be the only photograph I would carry with me of any of my family. When I replied to Helen telling her this she sent a message back saying that this had made her cry. I replied that it didn't matter, as I already knew what the rest of them looked like. I was glad when she replied that this made her laugh.

The Isle of Man team had told me that they were stopping nearby in another hotel and that perhaps we could all have dinner together, which seemed like a good idea to me. However I got a message from one of them to say that they had been delayed and would be late in arriving. I arranged for them to let me know when they got to their hotel so that I could drive over and meet them, which they did. It was only a quick visit but at least we managed to get some introductions in and finally put real faces to the names we had been reading on Facebook.

All in all an eventful day, what with one thing and another, but finally I was tucked up in bed and trying not to be so excited that I couldn't sleep.

Saturday 24th March 2012
Heathrow airport to Tromso, Norway
N 69° 38'921 E 18° 57'444

My alarm goes off at 0310 the following morning and I've had about 5-½ hours sleep. Time to get up and go, well get up, the go had gone at that hour!

Surprisingly, once I am awake things move along without hitch. I am first at the airport am checking in when the Isle of Man crew arrive. Boy do we all look apprehensive.

As well as we Northerners there are also Jess, Chris and Neil who are all from the London area. Neil, like me, is alone, but it turns out he has previously met the other two.

For the last 16 years I have been directing a programme called the Rotary Youth Leadership Awards (RYLA) where young adults (their average age for the event is 17) who have demonstrated leadership potential to their community, school, youth group or employer, are nominated and attend a course run by Rotarians. The course is designed to improve their potential by giving them the opportunity to experience leadership of their peers in a series of exercises designed to challenge them. Group and individual feedback sessions follow each exercise. I am proud to have been associated with this programme, as it has given me the opportunity to work with and help some of the best prospects for the future that our local communities have produced.

The exercises we stage are based on outdoor activities, I must stress we do not teach outdoor pursuits but use the outdoors as it is a great leveller of personal abilities. We also have classroom sessions on the theories of team dynamics, personal development and other, allied, topics. One feature of the course is that there are 32 participants drawn from all over Yorkshire, none of whom have met before they arrive at the venue.

So here I am at Heathrow airport and I now find myself in a situation not unlike that that of the RYLA participants. I watch as the team dynamics start to develop and interesting it is to experience, rather than observe and control. After all these years of teaching it I think it will be interesting to see the outcome from the other side.

Funny thing these team dynamics. When I arrived at the airport I used the self check-in and selected seat 14C because it showed A & B as occupied. When I was at the hotel with the Isle of Man group I was told that some of them were booking in online so I gambled that they had taken the occupied seats and that I would be sat next to someone from our party. It turned out that the A & B seats were empty which left me sat on my own. I know that this has happened by chance, but do the rest of the group? What kind of message does it send to them about me?

The check-in system for SAS at Heathrow is of the self-service variety. I had to enter my booking reference and passport number, select my seat and then print out the luggage tags. From here we then have to queue up to deposit the luggage at another desk. This begs the question why have a self-checking in system if you then have to join a queue? This gives us the opportunity to start conversations and make introductions especially as we have to gather and wait while we are processed.

Mike arrives and straight away approaches and asks if I will watch his hand luggage while he goes through the baggage drop. I suddenly realise that he is wearing the same coat as me, and now has a beard, which makes us look like a team. The others start asking me questions about where we need to go, how long will it take us to get there, about the equipment they have and what will be issued.

Some of these I can answer as a result of travelling with SAS before; some from my background interest in Artic exploration. Others I have to admit to not having a clue. I realise that there are some barriers need breaking at an early stage and that we need to get to know each other fast.

The Isle of Man contingent have a common aim in raising funds for their Children's Home and have a variety of careers, the biggest contingent is from the Electricity Generating Company, with roles as diverse as IT support and Human Resources. The Post Office and Ambulance Service are also represented. Neil is a medical student in London, Chris is a self-employed electrician and Jess is an administrator in a small company. All in all we are a diverse bunch but with a common interest.

During these initial conversations I hear a familiar accent and learn that Kathryn is not really a 'Manx' but is from Leeds. We soon end up swapping tales of places we know as she used to live not far from me.

Overall it seems like we have a good bunch of people. A lot of waiting in Airports in store for us but that is compulsory with modern travel, it all seems to be about hurry up and wait, get searched, queue up, hurry up again and then drink horrible coffee at an inflated price.

Eventually the flight leaves Heathrow and then comes the first surprise of day, the coffee is free on the flight. I wonder how long luck like this will last. We arrive in Oslo, Norway and as usual I am surprised by how relaxed Scandinavian airports seem to be, none of the mad hustle and bustle of UK and USA venues. Then comes the first problem, Neil from London has managed to have his luggage lost by the airline, which is not a good omen. Team leader Mike stays in the baggage area to help Neil and I go out to find everyone else standing in the public area, just waiting. I suggest that we go and check in for the next flight and then take up residence in a coffee bar, which is accepted by them all (good old team dynamics again). So we re check the baggage for the Tromso flight and file through security.

Easy really and made easier by the coffee bar being just inside the doors giving us an ideal place to sit and wait for Mike and Neil. Then up pops the next problem. One of the ladies, I shall call her 'Elsie', from the Isle of Man, manages to get turfed out of the security queue because she has taken a trolley with her. This, despite a sign that says 'do not take trolleys past this point'. This is compounded when she tries again and goes through the international departure gates into the wrong area. We only find this out about 45 minutes later when she is delivered to us by a security man with a look of real exasperation on his face. Mike and Neil turn up from the baggage claim area without Neil's bag. Still we have another 3 hours to kill, so things could improve.

With all this time to fill a walk about is called for, all 300 yards of it and back again. Past the food stalls selling Pizza at £30 for a normal sized one and beer at £8 for just over half a pint. Having been to Norway before I knew it was a little on the expensive side, but not to this expensive. Somehow we fill the time and file onto the flight for more, thankfully, free, coffee.

We arrive in Tromso to be greeted by slate grey skies and loads of snow on the ground. It alternates between snowing and sleet as we load the trailer and climb on the bus to travel to the Vilmarkssentre, the base of our tour guides. The weather soon changes though, it gets dark and the snow falls thick and fast. Welcome to 350 kilometres above the Arctic Circle. Neil is still without his luggage.

The journey only takes 15 minutes and it is a surprise to see people doing 'normal' everyday things. A young mum pushing a pram, a chap digging a hole in the road, that sort of thing. It is only when you look closely that you see that the pram has skids not wheels and the man with the shovel also has a big blow torch to keep defrosting the ground! When we arrive at the base for the expedition, The Vilmarkssentre, a wall of sound immediately confronts us. The sound of hundreds of dogs barking. Otherwise it looks like any number of Outdoor Pursuits centres I have visited over the years, lots of wood cabins, vans and minibuses apparently abandoned and every door labelled with the name of someone famous. In this case famous in Norway!

After dumping our bags in the equipment hut we stretch our legs and get to meet the dogs. They live in kennels that are designed for two dogs with a dividing wall between the two sleeping areas, the dogs being paired for work and living together is obviously part of their teamwork ethic. It is quite surprising to find that they are quite friendly which I did not expect of something that is regarded as a semi domesticated animal, not quite wild but certainly not the hearth rug variety that I have at home. They all bark and howl all the time when we are about and what a noise it is, I just hope they become quiet when it is bedtime.

We meet the Lead Guide, Tore, and he immediately reminds me of my friend Paul Findlay who I have worked so closely with on the Rotary Youth Leadership Awards for the last 16 years: precise, careful, to the point, talks about teamwork, teamwork, teamwork and how we are one big team and lots of small ones. This is a man who has a passion about what he does and wants to share it and has some stories to tell. The first thing that I noticed is that he has lost 6 fingers below the first joint and when asked about it merely says 'frostbite'; the story will obviously have to wait to be told once he is certain the work of the day is done.

Lessons then ensue on tent erection and cookers. There is plenty of scope for frustration with them but still it adds to the adventure. We are issued with the arctic clothing, boots and gloves needed for the trip, which necessitates a repack. What a marathon session that is and still I am not sure I have it right! But then nor is anyone else so I am in good company.

We have dinner, reindeer stew, and do a bit more on the packing and preparation of kit when suddenly there are cries of 'Northern Lights' and we dash outside to see a break in the clouds and a bright green curtain shimmering in the sky. The magic lasts about 5 seconds and the cloud covers over again. I hope this is a good omen for the rest of the tour. We bed down for the night in the same hut we ate in and it is beginning to sink in just what I have let myself in for; 6 nights in the company of strangers in tents. We may have a wooden floor and roof tonight but are still in sleeping bags with a coat as a pillow. I find it surprisingly comfy with air mattress and mat, especially as I haven't roughed it like this for a considerable number of years.

All too soon it is 06:00 and we are on the move again.

Sunday 25th March 2012
Singnaldalen to 1st Camp – N 69° 4'465 E 20° 8'515
Distance covered – 15 Kilometres

In short order we are up and about and tucking into breakfast of muesli, porridge and sandwiches with coffee. We put our bedding away and then have one last attack on the bags. I now work on the theory that I will take my big holdall, not my rucksack, not so I can take more but so I have it in one place and can get at it easily. I am also starting to accept that if I don't have it, I must do without it. I make a decision that I will only take a minimum amount of spare clothing and resolve that I can survive the week in the same clothes.

At 8:45 I can hear the dogs getting excited as loading up begins. I see a young woman reeling the dogs in on their kennel lines and then wrestling them to the van. She holds them by their collars at the scruff of the neck and keeps their front legs off the floor. The dogs bounce along and bark loudly, she smiles and offers me a cheery good morning as she strides by. She has obviously done this before.

Loading the dogs is the noisiest process I have ever witnessed, they are all barking to get attention and seem to be saying 'Take me, Take me'. When placed in the travel kennels they bark as though celebrating. There has been a steady snowfall since we got up and the skies are leaden and grey. The benefit of this is that it is not as cold as might have been expected, only about -1C.

So far the first day has been like at the airport, lots of hurry up and wait, while the professionals do their job. Eventually we set off and travel in a mini bus to the starting point, via the airport to see if the lost bag has been recovered. Much to Neil's delight it has, all he has to do now is get into his own kit and give back all the stuff he has had to borrow. The dogs, sleds and all the other equipment follows on in a specially constructed vehicle with a trailer. 17 sleds and over 100 dogs don't seem to have made any impact on the locals as we pass through the Tromso and some smaller villages on the way. Nobody looks as it passes and the kids don't point at it. Must be a fairly common sight in these parts then.

It takes about 2 hours to get to the set off area, which is a car park at the start of the trail that leads up into the mountains. It seems that we will be following an established route that is used all year round by hikers, dog sleds, snowmobiles and ski tourers. We all pitch in to unload the sleds and park them in a neat row at the side of the parking area. We then all line up in our tent groups, it's a bit like first day at school when you get shown where to hang your coat and shoe bag. One of the staff comes down the line and asks us for our personal weights and then tells us each to take a sled and move it to an area for loading. We are then called up by group to collect the food allocation, which comes in a large clear plastic crate with a snap on lid. One crate for each team member and neatly balanced out so that we are each carrying a third of our allocation. Then comes the cooking equipment and fuel, tent, line for securing the dogs at night, shovels and most importantly the food for the dogs.

I also have the bag for my personal spare kit, snacks, cameras, sleeping bags and mats and as Mike approaches me with the team first aid kit I look at the small mountain of gear at the side of my sled and wonder if it will all fit. Then I realise that it has to or it will be left behind. If I don't have it, I can't use it; if I don't need it, it doesn't go with me; there is no room for anything but the essentials. Finally as we are starting to make headway on the packing Tore comes to our group and gives us the Sámi tent that the group can use in an evening, giving us the good news that we are the chosen guardians of this piece of equipment. No problem, we will just repack our sleds to accommodate it and redistribute a few dozen items in the process.

After we have managed to get everything in and pack away any discarded items for transport back to the centre we manhandle the sleds into lines for harnessing up. Quite a science to this it transpires. Starting from the back, which is me, the sled is lined up, the main pulling line is laid out, the ground anchor is put out and then secured by kicking it into the snow. The next sled is positioned so that it is about 1 metre in front of the end of the hauling line and then a rope, that is attached to the back of the sled frame, is tied to a loop on the front of the pulling line. This is then repeated with the next sled and our three-man tent team is set up. This is checked by the team leaders and adjusted where needed and we are told that this is how we do it every morning when we get ready to set off. The manhandling of the sleds was quite easy on this nice flat car park. I don't suppose it will always be that way.

We are next issued with the dog harnesses which we lay out alongside the pulling line. Then the fun starts. 100 dogs have to be got out of the travelling kennel and taken to the sled and handler that they have been allocated to. As soon as the dogs realise that this is happening they start the barking and howling again. It's like watching kids in the playground being picked for the football teams "Me, Me, I can do that, I'm good at pulling" is what they seem to be shouting. Either that or "Lets get on with it I want to run"

This is our first close up encounter with the dogs and it is soon apparent how powerful they are, despite looking slender. The recommended method of handling the dogs is to hold the collar tight and keep the dogs front legs off the ground, just like we had seen the staff doing at the centre. The dogs then bounce alongside you on their back legs pulling as they go in their eagerness to get harnessed up. We deliver them to the sleds, starting with the dogs at the front of each team, leaving the individual handlers to harness up. As this is repeated the number of people collecting dogs from the vehicles gets less and less as they are harnessing up, so that by the time it gets to Tony, Rod and I we are left with each other. We start to gel as a team over this and soon get into a routine of two of us fetching the dogs while the other harnessed them. This helps each of us bond with our own dogs and get proficient at the task.

The number of dogs allocated is calculated on body weight and equipment carried and I work out that overall the sled, equipment and me weigh in the region of 225 kilos, I am allocated 6 dogs while some members of the team are obviously lighter so are only allocated 5. My dog team, from the front position, are called Toyota, Audi, Bison, Tracker, Volvo and Subaru. These are the positions that they work in at all times as they each have a role that they are trained for. Toyota and Audi are female and are the leaders, they pick the route to follow and set the pace; Bison and Tracker are male and are only about 15 months old, they are still training so get put in the middle to be shown how to go on; Volvo and Subaru are also male and the two biggest dogs in the team. They are the powerhouses that get the sled moving and pulled round corners. The dogs are always harnessed up in the same order, front to back and then taken off in reverse. This is so that the line stays taught at all times and so that the dogs are always in the right order. In the set off area this has been quite a challenge, on the trail it would get more difficult.

The guides come and check that everything is in order and that we are ready to start and give us a few last minute instructions. We have to apply the brake on the sled and make sure we can reach the line tied to the sled behind us and that we can reach the collar of one of the lead dogs behind us. This is so that we can hold onto the team and stop them from going forward until we are ready. I don't have anybody behind me at this time so that is one thing less to worry about as I seem to be running out of hands and feet for all these tasks. Finally we are told to check that we can reach the ground anchor. Simple enough, yes? No.

As I reach down to the ground anchor my foot slips off the brake and because I am bent over I cannot see that Rod in front of me has untied the line from his sled to my dogs and isn't holding onto them. The dogs surge forward and as I am holding the sled with one hand and the anchor with the other involuntarily pull it out of the snow allowing the whole assembly to shoot forward dragging me with it! I manage to throw the sled onto its side and Tony catches the dogs stopping them from going further. This makes me the holder of the record for fastest falling off. Not a record I am proud of but someone has to do it. I was to learn that it would not be the last fall of the day or the whole trip and I would not be alone, not by a long way.

Dignity recovered and everything put back on an even keel, we set off. The dogs are released and surge forward. The sled glides along and I can feel every bump and lump in the snow surface, what a thrill! I can hardly believe it and with a small tear in my eye I say to myself, "I'm doing it, I'm really doing it at last".

The first Km or so is all stop-start as we get used to brakes. Another skill is turning the sled which is like riding a motorcycle. To get it to turn you have to put your weight onto the runner of the direction that you want to go in and then lean out. Sometimes quite a long way which involves hanging on with an iron like grip, not easy when the trees are overhanging and VERY close at times. It is very physical and I'm soon in a sweat and aching with hanging on. So much for the people that said, "I suppose all you do is just stand there and let the dogs pull you". I am soon grateful for the gym sessions and the training programme that was worked out for me.

I fall off another four times but nothing serious and soon have the hang of righting the sled, recovering my dignity and setting off again. We are travelling constantly uphill but the dogs just live to run and pull, even when the sled is on its side! I can't wait to see what happens when we reach the flat.

Just short of the summit we stop. Originally it had been to gather everyone into a tighter line but a small disaster befalls 'Elsie', who got off her sled and promptly fell through a snow bridge into a stream that was hidden from view. She gets quite wet and has to be pulled out and Tore declares that we will stop to make sure she will be OK. We have only done about 15 Km, which is not as far as we should have done but the safety of a team member overrides all other considerations. The first job is to tether the dogs, which is quite an effort. First we have to lay out the line in as straight a line as possible and fasten it between two trees so that not only is it tight and secure but so that there is room along the line for the dogs to move about a little. Their movement is restricted to a small arc defined by the length of chain attached to their collars but still they need to be away from trees and rocks.

The difficult part of all this is when first moving from the hard packed trail onto the soft snow, sinking up to the mid thigh is normal. This continues until several trips have been made and the snow has been packed down. Even then it is not stable enough to be depended on as a firm walking surface. If we thought that wading through this stuff hauling a metal hawser is hard, when we have to do it whilst holding a 20 to 25 KG dog that still has enough energy to bounce about on its back legs at the end of the day, we find out just how hard it can be.

I start to get organised with my tent mates Rod and Tony, and who are both just turning 50 and so closer to my age than the others. We form a line to string the hawser and then pass the dogs up our little human chain, which means that we can have a short rest and not get too hot and bothered. Of all the things that I have read about Polar and Arctic regions every author speaks of the dangers of sweating. Simply put if you sweat your under clothes get wet and then they can freeze, which can lead to body temperature problems and hypothermia. Not a good idea and why it is recommended that everything is done at a measured pace; referred to as the 'Polar Plod' by Ranulph Fiennes in his account of his walk across the Antarctic in his book 'Mind over matter'.

Unfortunately the last 2 of my dogs will not fit on our line so I have to take them to the next line and, worse luck, the guys that put it up didn't heed my plea to be left room at the end nearest to me so I have to trudge through some really deep snow to avoid walking past a line of dogs that had got settled. It turned out not to be the last time that this happened as at every stop but one they did the same, at least on the last two nights they had the good grace to feed my dogs for me to save me an extra trek.

After the dogs are tethered Tony, Rod and I have the stove going in no time and we get started on pitching the tent. We get on well, to say that we have only just met, which helps with the tasks we have to undertake. We all take a job and get on with it. On reflection it was probably our relative age and experience that contributed to our approach, we accepted each other's decisions and suggestions and as a result the camp was set up and we were having a brew long before anyone else. The best way to describe our actions is to say 'we don't committee, we do'.

I get elected as tent cook and set about our boil in the bag rations with all the aplomb of any fancy restaurant chef, well I think so anyway. Dinner that night is lasagne with noodles followed by chocolate biscuits and coffee. I doubt that any of the so-called posh places could beat not just the food but also the ambience. Sitting on a plastic storage bin in the open air, with snow falling, eating food straight from the bag and then making coffee with the water that was used to boil the bags, making sure that they didn't burst in the process although I doubt we would care, is an experience that money simply could not buy.

At this point I am about to sleep in a tent for the first time in almost 40 years, the last time being the same time of year but in The Yorkshire Dales while on an Outdoor Pursuits course as a Police Cadet, and at the end of that experience I said I would never do it again. Rod just said "I can't believe I'm in a tent, in winter, above the Arctic Circle in Norway". No, neither can I!

Having struggled out of the bulky outer clothing and then into a jumper and some long wool socks I wriggle into the sleeping bag and get settled for the night. I am sharing my bed with the box of batteries and my cameras. The sleeping bag has pockets specifically designed for this task and it is the only way of ensuring that they will 'live' through the night as, if they are left on the sled the cold will just cause the batteries to discharge and the cameras to seize up.

It strikes me as being strange that despite my assertions of years ago I don't miss the comforts of a hotel or home. I don't know whether I accept the situation as part of the experience or am actually enjoying the simplicity of it all. Time will tell. Whilst not feeling cold as such it is certainly noticeable even with the equipment we have been provided with. I can only imaging what it must be like in the real Polar Regions and have an even stronger desire to visit them. One day I will make it but for now at least I'm a bit nearer than I was 50 years ago!

Monday 26th March 2012
1st Camp to 2nd camp – N 68° 57'842 E 20° 21'182
Distance covered – 20 kilometres

The night has not been as cold as I thought it might be but then again we did have all the right gear. The surprising thing is how well a thin nylon tent has kept out the wind and snow. The sleeping bag was well up to the task and the mats we had were great. That is until we collectively rolled over and ended up on the gap in between them, a cold hip soon wakes one up and causes a bit of shuffling to get back on a warm bit. Overall we actually got a good nights sleep despite Tony's snoring, which of course he denied. His hobby is sailing large yachts and a side effect is his ability to go to sleep in about 10 seconds flat, which I envy right from the start. We are all awake at 05:30, just like home for me and the others it seems; must be the age thing again. We decide to get up at 06:00 having had a chat about this and that for a while and soon had the stove going for coffee followed by breakfast of porridge and bread that has been held near the cooker to pretend that it is toast.

The morning ablutions are a real introduction to the outdoor life, Norwegian style. The guides have impressed on us the need to respect the environment and to make sure that we leave nothing that will harm or blemish. Solid and liquid waste is not a problem, as long as we do it away from the watercourse, but the toilet paper is another thing. In the low temperatures it will not rot down and when the snow melts will be a lastingly offensive memory of our passing, so the suggested method is to burn it. Now, I don't know how many people reading this have tried to burn used toilet tissue but, trust me, it is not easy.

After a fairly leisurely breakfast, which gave us time to chat and get to know each other better, we start to clear up and by 08:45 we are fed, packed and ready to go with just the tent to take down. We are far more advanced than the rest of the group. Then the word comes down the line that we will be delayed in setting off because 'Elsie' has decided that the challenge is too much for her and that she will be turning back. Given her performance in the airport and the first stop it is the right decision for her to take. I learned later that she had tried to persuade one of the other women to give up as well, I am equally sure that this would have been the wrong thing to do, we all have to make our own choices in life, influence and persuasion have their place but if you have accepted a challenge and stated an aim then you should see it through. If you decide on abandonment then it is wrong to try and persuade others to follow you when you give up.

We have a lengthy delay while her gear is reallocated, her sled turned and the dogs shared between the guides so that she can be escorted back to the start point. It is probably a bit of luck that we had only gone a short distance. Still, having to allow for Torquill to take her back, wait for the other team members to come from the centre to collect her and then leave enough time for him to catch us up means that we don't set off for a while yet. When we do, we have to follow a shortened route which leads to, time and distance lost having to be made up in the following days.

It has proved to be a hard going day, some very technical paths through the tree line followed by a climb up to the top of a mountain, descend down the other s ide and then climb another. Norwegian topography at its best!

Dogs are like cars in reverse, quiet when running noisy when stopped! On the occasions when we stop, because someone has fallen or just to get the group to bunch up the dogs start to bark and howl. They seem to be complaining that they are not working and that we need to get a move on. It seems to last about 10 minutes and then they take a time out and have a rest, even to the point of curling up and going to sleep. Until another dog somewhere in the line barks or howls for some reason and then they all spring back into life and join in the chorus. It gets so loud that it is difficult to hear anything else, not that we are close enough to hold a true conversation with the next person.

It snows all day and at times the conditions are near whiteout and the actual trail is hard to see. Well for me it is, the dogs seem to know exactly where to go even when it is unclear to me. Most of the trail is hard going. Uphill is hard, level is difficult, and down is just scary, especially when 'down' suddenly appears. Even when visibility is OK it is still hard to judge how steep a drop is and just when it levels out.

Conditions are such that there is no discernable scenery but the experience is one of, ' I have never felt so alive'. There can be very few occasions in life when you are left so alone with your own thoughts whilst concentrating on the basics of staying upright and hanging on, a challenge in itself in these conditions, and being able to just forget about everything else. Even after two huge falls as a result of not being fully in control and letting the sled run away from me, I knew I had lots to learn and set myself the goal of remaining focussed and not just letting the dogs and the sled take me where they wanted to go.

Mind you it is not all about the scenery, dog and sled control, it's about the experience and let me tell you some experiences will scar you for life. Watching a dog empty its bowels while it is running and pulling a sled is something that cannot be unseen (unfortunately). Mind you, I have to admire their dedication to task; they really do just want to run and pull the sled and that is their sole focus. As a team of six they work well together but they also function in pairs within that overall structure. The two lead dogs set the pace and choose the route, the middle two are still learning as they are only young dogs but still pull their weight and provide their part of the motive power, while the two at the back provide the real hard work of getting things moving after a halt, turning corners or just simply getting up the steep bits. The others have a part to play and we wouldn't go anywhere unless they work together, but the back two, or wheel dogs, really are the powerhouses.

Today saw me getting to grips with the actual sled driving and as I discovered on the first day it is a very physical activity. The basics are simple, left foot on left runner, right foot on right runner, hands grip handle. The brake is a simple press down and drag in the snow to cause a build up that makes it progressively harder for the dogs to pull until they stop. It actually doesn't get much more complicated than that, well until you start to move that is! The dogs set off with a tremendous jerk that causes the whole sled to jump up; this requires a grip of iron and a feat of balance that would do a tightrope walker proud. Then the track undulations have to be contended with, some of which are a drop of about a metre or so, but mostly it's like running on corrugated iron without the benefit of it being in a regular pattern. Add to that, that due to the snow falling and the dogs covering the immediate area of view the actual trail is almost impossible to see and therefore predict. You are now starting to get a picture of how difficult it can be to maintain balance. My orthopaedic surgeon obviously did a good job on the knee replacement as it never hurts or, more importantly, fails.

I have previously described the method of causing a sled to deviate from a path or turn it to follow the dogs round a corner. Yes there are some even in the middle of nowhere, requiring the rider to lean out like a motorcyclist. Mostly this manoeuvre is used to assist the sled travel in a straight line whilst traversing a slope, as without this action the sled would run at an angle behind the dogs making it hard for them to work efficiently. It would also run the risk of the sled being at an angle to the direction of travel and therefore being toppled over by a combination of the forces at work. Leaning involves using the whole body weight, balancing on one runner and gripping the handle. Gripping is a mild description, hanging on like grim death would be nearer.

Amongst all this physical activity the rider has to watch the dogs as they run, to see that they are not limping or in distress. Not an easy task with 24 legs flailing away as we move forward at about 10 KPH. The track they are running in is watched to see that there is no sign of blood from feet that may have been cut on ice or exposed stones. The dogs have to be watched to see that they take a 'drink' of snow every so often and to see that there is no sign of blood from their mouths, again indicating cuts, or of vomit from over exertion.

The most important task is to keep the centre pull line as straight and taught as possible. The dogs are all fastened to this line and run close to it, so as well as being the main translator of their effort into forward motion, it is a method of controlling them. To assist this they are also fastened from their collars to the centre line to stop them straying too far off to one side. The dangers of not maintaining the line's rigidity become apparent very early on. If slack the dogs can move in different directions from each team of two, thereby losing forward motion. It can also get under the dogs and between their legs so that when it goes tight again it will pull up under their groin or shoulder and can cause an injury.

Going downhill presents a special challenge as the weight of the sled causes it to overrun and catch the dogs up which has the effect of releasing the weight from them, allowing them to run faster.
This causes the sled to jerk as they take up the slack making it overrun even more and the process starts again. To counteract this the rider has to brake to hold the sled back but, of course, this puts weight onto the dogs' pull causing them to pull even more, again resulting in jerks and overruns. At the same time the rider has to maintain balance, steer, watch for snow banks or holes. Inevitably this all goes wrong every so often and one ends up in an undignified heap on the ground.

Falling off is an art as well as this also requires a set of skills not previously acquired by me. Without a rider to apply the brakes the dogs will simply keep running and follow the trail/team in front until either A) Caught and stopped
Or
B) They get tired/bored and stop of their own accord

So when, and please note the lack of the word 'if', the rider falls off they must hang on to the sled and pull it over onto its side so that it digs in and brakes the forward motion. Continuing to grip the sled is a must as even on its side it can still be pulled some distance and could cause problems for recovery. This usually results in being pulled in a most undignified fashion for what is a short, but seems like a very long way.

To get going again the procedure is as follows: -
Set the ground anchor out and make sure it is firm.
Put one foot onto the brake pedal and push it into the fully applied position, this will be under the sled, as it has nothing to bite into.
With the other leg and both hands pull the sled into an upright attitude keeping pressure on the brake so that it bites into the ground.
Keep a firm grip on the sled, as the dogs will start to pull as soon as they feel the resistance release and the ground anchor may be pulled out.
Keep pressure on the foot brake and check that everything is still attached, the dogs are OK and that you still have all your limbs.
Checking limbs is easy, as they will now ache from the fall and the exertion of getting the sled, and yourself, upright. If you can feel the ache they are still attached.

Once everything is ready, keep the foot brake on release the ground anchor, take a firm hold, release the foot brake and set off with the now familiar jerk from the dogs. Don't forget that whatever it was that caused the fall might still be in the immediate area so be ready to be unbalanced all over again.

As the instructors on the Police advanced driving courses used to drum into us 'Concentration aids anticipation' a statement that applies to a 6-dog power sled as much as 150 horse power patrol car.

So much for the 'I suppose all you will do is just stand there' brigade then. Yes, it is hard work but it is surprising how satisfying it is to pit yourself against the elements and the challenge of doing something that is as far from your normal routine as can be imagined. Perhaps the simplicity of it all is the real attraction? It may sound a little contrived given the well organised nature of the event, the marked trails, the rest of the team and the competency of the guides, but there is the ever present scent of danger around what we are doing. There is also the connection to a past when this was the only method of long distance travel in snowbound conditions. To say that I am enjoying myself is the understatement of a lifetime.

The climb up the mountains affords us some spectacular scenery, or would if not for the snow that keeps falling and being whipped up by the wind. At one point we are going across a mountainside at about 10 KPH with a wind from the side at about 15KPH when I discover that there is a gap between the fur trim and the hood of my parka. This allows a sneaky little icy blast to hit the only spot on my face that is uncovered. High up on my right cheek between the neck warmer and the bottom of my goggles. I discovered that the trim was held on with press-studs and that a couple had come undone and try as I may I couldn't manage to fasten it up while on the move, so my face became steadily colder and colder.

I never thought that I would be at risk from frostbite but the sensation of a cold patch of skin is such a sensitive area made me aware of just how soon it could happen. I can only imagine the pain it would cause. I have read so many times about polar explorers suffering frostbite and the appalling injuries it can cause and I now have a very tiny insight to their suffering. Scott in his diary on the fateful trip to the South Pole describes the appearance of his comrades' feet, hands and faces as they steadily succumbed to the horrors of frostbite. Toes and fingers turning black, whilst noses and cheeks loose flesh, as it dies in the extreme cold. There are no words that can describe the pain they must have suffered, as they had to continue walking and erecting tents, not to mention trying to undertake delicate tasks such as trying to repair equipment or get stoves going to make food.

Our lead guide, Tore, has lost most of his fingers to frostbite, although the stump ends look neat. He obviously had the best medical attention possible but there is no doubt in my mind that it was painful when it happened, excruciating when it took hold and soul destroying when the results are viewed. I marvel at how he copes but then, that's what people do, we cope with adversity. To do otherwise is just to lie down, admit defeat and become a victim.

As we traverse the mountains there is almost no sign of the hand of man to be seen. Aside from the poles that mark the route, when we are following one that is, there is nothing. No fences, electricity poles, mobile phone towers, buildings, vehicle tracks, roads or even aeroplanes in the sky. Then there is the absence of noise. Aside from the wind swirling round my hood and the swish of the sled runners there is no other sound at all. No cars, trucks, snowmobiles, aeroplanes, TV sets, radios, mobile phones and, much to my relief, no emergency vehicle sirens! The down side is that because of the way we travel there is no opportunity for conversation with my team mates either. As a 'people person' who likes to interact I thought that this might be a problem at first but soon find myself content with my own thoughts and the concentration of the task in hand.

We come down off a mountainside and pull up at what will be our camp for the night. The snow is extremely deep as we pull off the main track and the dogs merely slow down and pull us through the soft powder. Tony, Rod and I are directed to an area that is well back from the main track and as we drop the ground anchors and step off the sled runners we start to sink in to about knee depth.

This is no bar to our normal routine; secure the dogs with the ground anchor and tie them off to the back of the sled in front, give them a quick check over, and look for a tethering site for the dogs.

As we start to put the line out we find that we are walking, if that is the term, in thigh deep snow at times. The teamwork approach for setting up the tether is employed again and we soon are sorting our dogs out to be tied up for the night. Once again my last two are at the far end of the other teams' line and getting them to it really is hard work as I have to make a new path to the space they have left me.

We get the dogs bedded and start flattening an area for the tent, simple enough; we just trudge in a small square until it is big enough and hard enough to pitch the tent on. As Rod and Tony put the tent up I set about making a brew for us as only two people are needed for that task and we are all ready for a hot drink.

When we first met I had told both of them about my replacement knee and the weakness of my lower left leg as a result. The guides tell us that there is a source of fresh water in a nearby stream and that they would lead us to it. Tony and Rod tell me to stay at the camp because of my leg and insist when I protest. They are right of course, I just didn't want to be seen as wimping out on a task. There is no point in getting injured and ruining the rest of the trip. We agree that I will get dinner going whilst they set off for water.

I set about melting snow and soon have two pans on the go and am able to get a boil in the bag meal going. I start to think that they have just given me a task that keeps me from getting hurt, which they have, but soon realise that what I am doing is just as important as all the other tasks we have to perform. A perfect example of teamwork at its best. Each member performing to the best of their ability to the overall benefit of the group without concern for their own personal needs, which are taken care of at the same time and as a direct result of the collaborative actions.

Not long after I have got started I look up to see that Tony has returned, but that he is not carrying any water. He tells me that he has turned back because the trail they are following is 'stupid'. When pressed he elaborates, explaining that the snow was equal in depth to that which we have just waded through to tether the dogs and pitch the tent and that the distance involved was much further than was originally described. It seems the countryside 'not far' is the same in Norway as it is in the UK. Add to this the fact that he knew just how long it would take to prepare water by melting snow so he decided that it was an experience that he did not need. For the benefit of my younger or more sensitive readers I have greatly paraphrased the language he used!

His description of the journey only serves to underline to me that they were right to insist on me not going. We sit and chat about this and that and start to learn about each other and our respective reasons for undertaking this challenge; this is in stark contrast to how we all spend the day, alone with our thoughts and a view of 6 dogs' backsides as the day rolls on. Once again I find food for thought in the situation and how difficult it must be for teams of people who undertake Polar Exploration on a professional basis. They spend time together in the planning, preparation and training stages, and then when it comes to the actual event they are on their own.

Ranulph Fiennes describes a similar situation in 'Mind Over Matter' when he describes being angry at Mike Stroud over the setting of the pace and navigating errors whilst on the move. He states that he allowed it to occupy his thoughts all the time while on the move. However he did not allow this to continue when they were together again. Here they were dependant on each other for setting camp and preparing food, dressing sores and repairing equipment. Not the same intensity as they experience but the principle is the same; individual thoughts become secondary to cooperation and collaborative tasks.

Rod gets back and is exhausted and extremely annoyed. It turns out that the walk was a very long way and was in deep snow at all times making an arduous trek into and unrelenting task. Again his verbal description has been censored! Tony and I make him a brew and instruct him to sit back and relax.

I put the finishing touches to the evening meal and we have a feast of boil in the bag reindeer stew and noodles. Fortunately neither of the others noticed that when I cooked the noodles I accidentally put two different flavour sachets (Beef and Chicken) into the pot at the same time. Wonderful what hunger does to disguise taste.

After some tidying up and sorting out of kit I make up my journal. The other two ask what it is I am writing about and I explain that it has become a habit of mine to keep a record whilst travelling, on the premise that 'it didn't happen if it isn't written down'.

I also explain that I am already booked to give talks about the challenge to various sponsoring rotary clubs and that my journal will form the basis of my notes for those and a full written record of the event. We decide that it is time for bed at 21:00 and get settled down. We chat for a while and learn a bit more about each other once we are in our sleeping bags but soon the exertions of the day catch up and we fall soundly asleep!

Tuesday 27th March 2012
2nd camp to 3rd camp – N 68° 44'260 E 20° 22'475
Distance covered – 55 Kilometres

I woke a couple of times in the night as the wind was quite strong at times causing the guy ropes to sing and the tent to flap somewhat. Not that alarming really as I have faith in the way we have pitched and lashed the tent down but still enough to wake me briefly. The wind died down but it obviously continued to snow, as when I look at the walls of the tent the snow is much higher up the sides than I recall it being when we set up camp. It has been surprisingly warm and comfy in the tent despite the weather conditions outside, a tribute to the equipment we have with us. My one concession to luxury has been the pillow I brought with me, I know it takes up quite a bit of room in the sled but when it is rolled into the hood of my sleeping bag I am every bit as comfortable as I am in bed at home. At first a couple of the team members laughed but when Tony found that his inflatable pillow lasted only the first night he said that he wished he had brought one. Certainly beats rolling up a jumper to use as a headrest.

During the night the snowstorm blew itself out and the temperature had dropped to well below zero, it was estimated at about -10C and as a result of the snow that had covered the tent the zips on the door have frozen up. Any water that had been left in bottles was now solid and all the gear on the outside has a crust of ice on it. It is just before 0600 as we get up and start to make a brew and have breakfast. Once again Rod, Tony and I have ourselves organised and have fed ourselves, filled the flasks, got the tent down and all the gear packed away, except the burner for one last brew, before there are signs of life from others.

This gives us the chance to relax before we start the exertions of the day. The weather this morning is sunny and clear and the view is fantastic. The valley we are in rolls away like a white carpet while the mountains we descended the night before rise up into the sky like jagged sentinels. The rock faces appear blue in the morning light while the snow has a pink tinge from the low angle of the sun. Again I am struck by the awesome splendour of nature, untouched, free and testament to the transient nature of man. This view has been like this for millennia and will be for many more to come. Few or millions may see this very view but it will stand and remain impervious to our schemes, dreams, cities and wars and will still be here long after we have completed our evolutionary journey or destroyed ourselves.

Suddenly I spot two ski trekkers coming into view from further down the valley, they just plod along at a steady pace dragging sleds with their gear on, the way that so many of my heroes undertook their explorations. As I watch them traverse our track and then steadily become smaller and smaller as they vanish into the distance I silently applaud their effort and commitment. Just the two of them against whatever the environment chooses to throw at them and a pace dictated by how they cope with it. I make a mental note that this is definitely something I want to try although I will really have to get fit for that one and I am not sure what the family will think when I tell them. I have no doubt that Pauline will try and persuade me that it is too hard, but only for about three mentions and will then support me as she always does.

I feel confident enough in my abilities with the sled to try out the video today and as I have time set about fastening it to the sled handles. A very Heath Robinson set up, using the Velcro harness supplied by the makers and a series of plastic cable ties looped round and over. I have tried to line it up so that it is pointing not just in the direction of travel but also as close as possible to the riders' line of sight. Of necessity it is at about waist height, but this should not affect the overall impact of the images. With no means of checking the recordings until I get to a computer and download them I have no way of viewing what I will have captured, all I can do is hope that it works.

When we pitched camp last night the snow was knee deep as usual since we had pulled off the main trail not just to be out of the way in case of snowmobilers coming past, apparently this is one of the areas that is traversed by groups who are out hunting the northern lights, but also so that we can be amongst the trees where we can tether the dog line. This morning, following the overnight snow fall, the depth has increased and even the areas that we had tramped down as we set the dogs out and pitched the tents has a deep covering again. This makes the task of manhandling the sleds into line and then harnessing the dogs a bit more of a struggle even with our, by now, well established team routine.

When set up it becomes apparent that to get onto the main trail again the dogs will have pull through this deep snow, as there is no actual track cut for our teams. Linus, the guide who has been at the back with us from the start wades through the powder to get Tony and his team pointed in the right direction and as he gets going I marvel at the sheer power of the dogs as they haul the outfit through snow that is a couple of feet deep. Rod sets off and then Linus calls me up. He takes hold of the front dogs and warns me not to step off the sled runners as I will just fall through the powder snow and be dragged off the sled, with that he points the lead dogs along the little track that has been cut and lets them run. If I thought watching the others set off was an impressive demonstration of dog power it is nothing compared to being directly behind them as they literally plough through the deep snow with the practised ease of being born to the task. For some reason they do not sink into the snow as I expected they would, I appreciate that they have their weight spread over 4 small pads rather than 2 big feet but I did think that, with the small surface area and the application of force, they would sink further than they do.

With an overall weight in excess of 200 kilos behind them in the shape of the sled and me the dog team set about the deep snow as though it was a walk along a city footpath. They almost seem unhappy when we have to stop after about 500 metres as we are getting ourselves into the travel line now we are back on the main trail. This gathering this morning takes longer than usual as the remaining sleds behind me have to struggle out of the camp and then we have to wait for Linus to get back to his team and come and take his place in the line.

We get started and it is not long before the blue skies of breakfast give way to grey clouds and it starts to snow again. Not just snow but also the wind picks up again and this time it is coming across our path making any exposed bits of face feel cold quickly. A bit of experimentation with the hood of the parka soon has this cured although peripheral vision is reduced to the black interior and the fur trim but this is much better than getting cold skin.

As we get into our stride the running is smooth as the trail is icy and polished by the wind. We are travelling uphill steadily with periods of traversing the mountain face as we described a circular route round a particular group. The only thing I miss is actually knowing where we are. I appreciate that the guides are familiar with the route and can navigate by experience alone but having access to a map would be nice.

I know that I keep saying this but it bears repetition; The dogs are magnificent they maintain a steady pace with the lead dogs dictating it and adjusting for the terrain, whether it is uphill, across the face, along a plateau or downhill they decide what is best for the team and the sled. It has been explained to us that they are bred for the task, rather than being a breed of dog that is used for the task, and it shows in their willingness to power along all day at a regular pace that simply eats up the distance.

The two middle dogs, Tracker and Bison, are younger than the others and are in training. This shows when they stop as they often pester the older dogs and nip at them. They soon get put in their place with a well-aimed snap of the jaws, or even a menacing growl, but being young they keep trying and keep being put down. One of the things they have a habit of doing is chewing the collar trace that fastens them to the centre line, not just when we stop but also when on the run. Apparently it takes some time for them to get used to having it on as it restricts their movement somewhat and keeps them in line with the others. It also helps maintain the team pace, as they have to keep up or get jerked about. This becomes a bit of an issue when one of the middle pair chews through a collar trace, he runs ok for a while but then decides that he wants to pause to answer the call of nature with a modicum of comfort. This does not end well, in short order he is run into by the wheel dog behind him and is pulled clean off his feet as his harness is jerked along by the centre line powered by the other 5 as they continue at their designated pace. As W C Fields said "I have never seen anything so funny as the misfortune of a friend" and my concern at the wellbeing of the dog is balanced with the humour of the situation.

As we carry on the weather gets worse and the snow turns to ice and hail which blasts at us. It never seems to be from behind us, it is either directly in our faces or at right angles. It is the side blasts that are the most uncomfortable as they are the one that find the little gaps in the hood or at the cuff of the sleeve if a mitten has been pulled on and the sleeve not properly tucked in.

At times we experience near whiteout conditions. The driven snow combined with the pure white surface and the uniform grey sky meld into one and any features in the landscape become smoothed out with no sense of depth or distance. There are times when the sled in front, which is about 100 metres away, cannot be seen nor the actual trail that the dogs are following. The trail is marked with posts, which are black with a red X on them, and at its worst the next one in the series cannot be seen. I trust the dogs to know that we are going in the right direction, but the terrain I am on is a mystery and cannot be made out at all. It can be seen as it passes under the back legs of the wheel dogs and just before it runs under the sled, which leaves little time to react to the humps and dips other than absorbing them with the legs and gripping the handle tight all the time.

As I ride along I consider that a ski run in a tourist resort being subjected to these conditions would have been closed by the patrols for the safety of the tourists. Another lesson in just how challenging this trip is and what an experience it has proved to be.

There is no let up in concentration even on the long straight bits when the visibility is good. There is still a sled to guide, dogs to watch, teams in front to watch and then the terrain changes. I literally cannot see a hole or bump until I am right on it. Occasionally there is small rocky outcrop pushing up through the snow, usually at a point where we are cresting a small ridge or starting to go down one of the many short, but quite steep slopes and these cause the sled to get seriously out of balance as one side is dragged round while the other runs smoothly. This leads to many falls for the team as a whole and soon these protuberances become known as a sexual geological formation or in plain although somewhat industrial English, a f***ing rock! I find that in these situations the best thing to do is let the dogs keep pulling so that we power through and try to balance and/or cling on to the sled and keep going.

Up to now I have taken the opportunity of having a drink or a bite to eat when we have stopped, to bunch up or when someone has fallen, but I am starting to become so confident in my handling of the sled and dogs that while on the long straight patches I allow myself the luxury of getting a drink of water, a chocolate bar or even a sandwich while still moving. I am starting to feel at home on the rig; mind you this does not prevent me having the odd fall that brings me back to my novice status in short order.

Overall the trip is proving to be hard not just physically but also mentally. Shifting balance all the time is nothing compared to not letting the mind wander, and that really is a challenge. With very little in the way of visual reference points, one snow covered mountain, plateau or slope is much the same as another, and no concept of location my mind starts to wander on occasions as I think about all manner of things. One topic I find myself drawn to frequently is the stark and untouched beauty of my surroundings which I contrast with places such as the slate mines in Blaenau, Wales where generations of quarrymen have successively raped the hillsides in their pursuit of profit leaving behind a gaping wound that will never heal. A lasting monument to mankind's greed and lack of concern for the environment.

I console myself by remembering that I am living one of my dreams and that it is in a way that is having little or no environmental impact as it is a method of travel that is as old as mans' need to hunt for food and/or satisfy the need to explore and see what is over the next hill, an activity that fits with nature not acts against it.

We traverse a long slope and then turn off the main track and head towards a ridge that we can see some 500 metres above us. As we crest it we find that we have stopped at the top of a mountain, which has a large bowl appearance as it is ringed with crests of small peaks and ridges. On a couple of these we can see huts in the distance but otherwise it seems to be a plain flat expanse of nothing. It is about 16:00 and we have been running for over 5 hours.

Tore gathers us together and declares this the end for the day and congratulates us on putting in 55 Kilometres, much more than normal at this stage in the expedition, and that this is due to catching up for lost ground and time. It has been a long hard drive but now that we have finished I feel elated at the success of it. We look round and see that there are some posts driven into the ground alongside the area we have stopped in and it dawns on us that this is a permanent tethering point. He then has a surprise for us, we are sleeping in huts tonight and don't have to pitch the tents.

It turns out that we have actually stopped on a lake that in summer is a favourite spot for fishing and that this is what the huts are, small 'hotels' that can be hired.

They are used in winter by groups such as ours, snowmobile tours, ski touring groups and even the odd fisherman or two that come up to do some ice fishing; they literally drill a hole in the ice to drop a line through. A strange hobby if you ask me.

Before we are taken to the huts there are still the dogs to attend to. The setting of the tether is comparatively easy as the snow is frozen hard and not very deep and the posts are set at just the right distance for the length of our lines. Once all the dogs are sorted out we have to feed them. Usually it is a case of dropping a lump of meat in front of each of them and letting them get on with it, but tonight will be different. Because of the distance we have covered today, and that tomorrow is planned to be even greater, the dogs get an extra ration of meat, a scoop of biscuits and a real treat, a bowl of water. Normally they just get fluid from eating snow but because of the extra food and the location having easy access to water they get it 'ready made' so to speak.

Of course with space on the sleds at a premium we only carry 25 bowls for the 100 dogs so it is necessary for us to set up a conveyor system of taking out meat, then the biscuits, then the water. A simple enough task? No is the quick answer! The dogs are just like diners in any restaurant, they all have their own preferences for food and service. Most immediately gobble down the lump of meat but there are some that seem aware that in this location they are being watched by us and wait until we move away before eating; as the biscuits are served in a bowl, most eat them straight from it, while others tip the bowl up and eat them from the snow covered ground. When it comes to the water, some of them sniff it and then ignore it, preferring to eat snow, while others lap it up like it will be taken away again if they don't drink it immediately.

This causes much hilarity as some people can be seen actually pleading with the dogs to eat or drink up so that they can have the bowl back for use by another animal. Tore has a simple method of dealing with this; he upends the bowl and takes it away when he wants to use it, none of this waiting about. It seems harsh but as I watch him it is obvious that he knows his dogs very well and exactly which of them eat in which fashion and that he is not denying any of them anything. I also see him walking the line, apparently checking on us but in reality he is checking his dogs and the way they watch him shows that he is the leader of their pack and that they would do anything for him.

The feeding routine takes longer than normal as could be expected. When we are satisfied that they are all well fed and settled down for the night we start on getting ourselves sorted out. We unpack the food and sleeping bags from the sled along with any personal gear we need and load it onto a big flat bed sled pulled by a snowmobile that Tore has produced from somewhere. The trip to the huts takes about 5 minutes and takes us over a crest and up a hill to what can only be described as a small village consisting of about a dozen small huts, a larger central 'reception and office' and a toilet block.
It reminds me of the place we stay at when we celebrate the Midsummer Festival in Sweden, with our friends George and Monica Smidelik and their family. We stay on the island of Tjurko on the Baltic coast. The only difference between our present location and Tjurko is that the toilets there aren't strapped down to stop them being blown away.

The huts have fixed cooking facilities, plates and cutlery, bunk beds, heaters and a table and chairs for us to dine off. Luxury indeed! Tony appears with a six-pack of beers that he has bought from the reception and we enjoy a cold brew. I quiz him on the cost, knowing how expensive Norway and Sweden are, and he declines to tell us simply stating 'We have earned it and won't be doing this again any time soon, so its worth it. Cheers'. Luxury abounds and we soon start to complain about being too hot!

Dinner that evening is a luxurious affair, the plates may be odd sizes and from differing dinner services, the cutlery has been sourced in the same way and when we find three cups that match we give a small cheer. The meal was still boil in the bag reindeer and veggies with a side order of noodles followed by chocolate biscuits and jam on bread but, and trust me on this, it was heavenly and afforded us the comfort of a table and chairs instead of sitting on a plastic box outside the tent.

After this exceedingly pleasant repast Rod delves into his bag and produces a bottle of port, with all the flourish of a magician plucking a rabbit from a hat. We are putting ourselves on the outside of this unexpected treat when there is a knock at the door and Tore joins us.

After a few pleasantries about how are we coping and how we are enjoying the experience, and I really do mean 'a few' as he is obviously of the opinion that if we didn't want to be there we would have turned back after the first night. We get the chance to talk to him about his experiences as a professional guide and adventure activities leader and, well talk about dark horse! His exploits would fill several books and many of them would make strong men go pale. It turns out that he has competed in and won the Finnmark Race, a 1000 Kilometre event across the top of Norway and Finland, which is billed as the coldest race on earth, and 4 of the 6 dogs I am using were included in the team. He has also competed in the Iditarod, which is the longest dog sled race in the world, covering 1750 Kilometres across the Alaskan wilderness. However, he has not always done it with a sled and full dog team, he actually holds the record for completing the course using one dog and skis. He had a support team in place to keep ahead of him replacing dogs and feeding him but still, it is one hell of an achievement.

It is now that he tells us the story of his missing fingers. As well as dog sledding, running marathons and all manner of other long distance outdoor activities he is also a climber of some note (why am I not surprised?) and has completed 7 of the worlds 8 highest peaks. It is peak number 7 that that caused the damage. In a very matter of fact way he tells of how he, along with his wife and best friend, were part of a team climbing the offending mountain in South America when a storm raged in and blew away all the tents and equipment, delivering a serious head injury to his friend in the process. He described how he dug a snow hole, then put his friend in a sleeping bag with his wife into the hole to keep him warm and alive while he set about recovering as much of the equipment as he could.

Despite a lull in the storm they could not go down the mountain and he elected to recover more equipment to make things safer for the descent. The storm returned and he was caught out by it. With his hands becoming seriously affected by frostbite as he continually searched for the equipment they needed. It was thought that his hands might recover once they were back in Norway, where they have a fair amount of experience dealing with this sort of thing, but that was not to be the case and after 6 months of treatment the only option was to amputate the affected digits leaving him with stumps on the whole of his left hand and only 2 fingers intact on his right. Was he bitter about it? Not in the slightest, he merely shrugs and says 'You must respect your environment' and 'It is no matter, I am alive'. Apparently if you ask his wife about his heroic efforts and his skill in keeping them all alive she replies 'That is what he is for'. And I complain about having to carry the shopping from the car!

We look forward to sleeping in a bed for the night but as soon as I lay down I start to feel distinctly uncomfortable. At first I cannot work out what is wrong, then it dawns on me; the lumps in the mattress are not being smoothed out like the ones in the snow, then the second stage kicks in, I am actually TOO warm! I am really glad that I am tired, not only because of the mattress but because Tony sounds as though he is sucking air into his lungs through a rubber tube with a flap on the end, this is well beyond the medical definition of snoring. And so ends another fantastic day.

I am just dropping off when suddenly we here one of the other tent team members shouting "NORTHERN LIGHTS" at the top of his voice. As one we leap out of bed and quickly climb into our outdoor gear and go outside to be faced with …. well something that is rather hard to describe but I'll have a go.

In the clear parts of the sky there is a grey curtain that hangs and moves very slowly, almost as though it is in front of an open window that is letting a light breeze in. The 'curtain' both has and does not have a visible texture. It is neither cloud nor smoke; vapour nor material; transparent nor opaque. It is ethereal in quality and at times appears not to be 'there' at all, that is until you look away to another area and then when you look back t has changed shape and moved. Sadly there are none of the bright green lights that are usually associated with this phenomenon as there is a very bright moon.

The only thing that spoils the experience is the 40 mph wind whipping up the ground snow and driving it at us! Now that we know that the 'lights' are about and that the weather is clearing a little we hope for better view tomorrow night. That and a reduction in the wind.

Wednesday 28th March 2012
3rd camp to 4th camp N 68° 22'076 E 20° 02'557
Distance covered – 60 kilometres

This morning we get up at 06:00 to be greeted by the most fantastic sunrise. Some wonderfully coloured skies; high cloud reflecting pink, purple and deep orange and what is more the wind has died down. As we look out it is obvious that during the night the snow has fallen again only this time, and probably because we are 650 metres above sea level, the wind has created some deep drifts and coatings on doors and porch roofs. Our cabin door has a serious pile of snow against it, which we need to dig away before we can make a trek to the toilet cabin. As the sun comes up we are treated to some glorious sunshine and blue skies followed by what is probably the strangest sight in my whole life; a small caravan being towed along behind a snow mobile. We found out later that it was being used by two of the previously mentioned ice fishermen and when I wander over for a closer look they show me the caravan with great pride. It contains all the mods cons of heaters, DVD player, generator and, most important of all, a measuring gauge stuck above the door so they know if it is OK to keep the fish they catch. I am under no illusion that I will ever manage to persuade Pauline to try this as mode of holiday transport even if she gets her own fishing measure.

We get started on cleaning up and packing and the team work kicks in again, getting things sorted out in record time giving us time for a sit down and one last brew in comfort.

We return to the sleds via the snow mobile and trailer and as we approach the line of dogs it is immediately obvious how much snow and wind there has been overnight with the drifts around the sleds and dogs. The sleds have a substantial covering of snow on top and are surrounded by drifts that have blown up against them making them look like little mountains. Once again I marvel at the fortitude of the dogs. Each dog has curled up into a tight ball and created a perfectly round basin of snow that has drifted up against them. The insulation properties of their own fur combined with those of the snow drift have allowed them a level of comfort that would never occur to us mere humans, it is absolutely amazing how they have adapted and can survive in these conditions.

We have another feeding session this morning, the same meat as always but with the rigmarole of biscuits and water like last night. I'm starting to feel like a waiter in the local animal shelter. As the dogs tuck in we start to pack the sleds again, this time we are taking on board extra dog food as we are told we have two big days ahead and two camp-out nights with no food depots.

As we are on a lake this is the only time that we have to clean up after the dogs, and I don't mean the washing up. Rod and I end up on dog poo duty. The truth is we volunteered because we had cleared the sleds of the drifted snow, had all our gear sorted out and packed away, and didn't want to just stand about and get cold. The task is to scoop up the worst lumps and put them in a plastic bag for more suitable disposal. The good news is that it is frozen solid and does not smell, well not too much! This little task leads us to sing a version of the ABBA song 'Super Trooper' (I shall allow the reader to insert their own words but the rhyme involves scooper, pooper and shovelling) This is promptly captured on video by various smart phone wielding team 'mates'; I can hardly wait for it to turn up on You tube.

After the clean up we get the dogs harnessed and we are all set for the day's journey. It takes quite some time to actually get going for the simple reason that the runners on the sleds have actually frozen to the surface. They are so secure that even when the ground anchor has been removed and with the dogs pulling for all they are worth nothing moves. With a few well aimed kicks at the runners and some heaving and straining on the handle the sled comes free with a loud snap but it does not set off in the normally smooth way as the runners have lumps of ice stuck to them. After a few metres these have smoothed off and the dogs settle into their distance-eating lope.

Like yesterday virtually as soon as we set off the blue skies vanish as a bank of cloud turns the skies grey. It is soon apparent that this morning will be a bit of a drag as the immediate terrain is a seemingly endless slope leading off towards the ridge on the far horizon. We settle into a steady uphill climb, which after about an hour turns into a traverse as we move across the face of the mountain. The snow holds off and there is almost no wind. This affords us some views that are barren, desolate and beautiful all at the same time. There is nothing to see but the rolling path in front of us, the slope down to the valley below us and the peaks above us and in the distance. It is so still and peaceful that I cannot help but think how the hand of man ruins almost everything it touches; this seems to be something that frequently comes to my mind.

The actual running is harder than can be imagined, with constant changes to balance, pulling on the sled to maintain it in a straight line so as not to slip down the slope we traverse, keeping the dog line tight and watching the dogs to see that they are running OK. Couple this with the occasional, and sudden, drop down a sharp incline, it is not just the physical effort but also the mental discipline needed to keep the level of concentration high enough to serve all the tasks undertaken at the same time.

By now I am confident enough of my ability on the sled to be able to take photos, eat a chocolate bar or sandwich or have a drink while on the move. Even with this newfound confidence there is no time to be bored or even blasé as the sled team in front can stop without notice, the rider can fall off unexpectedly or even disappear from view as they make a sudden descent. Every so often the terrain throws us a reminder that we are in a wild environment with some steep drops that usually have a large rock right in the middle of the track. The dogs avoid it of course but the sled never does and unless the rider has the balance abilities of a high wire artist it is another trip to view the ground at close quarters. Still with the number of times we fell off in the first few days we are all proficient, very proficient, at recovering and setting off again.

I have tremendous admiration for the people who undertake the long distance dog sled races, their level of fitness must be equal to that of any traditional athlete and their level of sustained concentration would astound a chess grand master. Their greatest skill is in the handling of the sled and dogs especially as they are alone for most of the time and only have their own abilities to rely on. When I fall off if something goes wrong there are the other team members and guides to help me, when they fall off they are alone.

We continue to make progress through this alien yet beautiful landscape when the air is filled with the sound of two stroke motors. We are in a high bowl like plateau created by a circle of peaks following our track when I see another track at exact right angles rising from my right and disappearing into the white horizon on my left. Shortly afterwards a group of snow mobile drivers come into view sounding like a nest of angry hornets. Tore at the front has halted and they pass across the front of us, then turn and give us a wide berth as they head off in the direction we have come from. Some wave, some don't, I suppose it depends how confident they are about controlling the machine. Or how friendly they are, miserable people can turn up anywhere, even in my private paradise.

Tore has decided that this is an ideal opportunity for a break so we stop for a few minutes, to have a drink and a sandwich. After a short while I see Tore start to move off when suddenly a snow mobile appears right in front of him and has to swerve to avoid a collision. I see Tore leap off his sled and launch himself at the driver. I can see him gesticulate but obviously cannot hear him, I really don't need to hear him as I can imagine the choice words he is using at the incompetence of someone who has nearly run into his dog team. When we stopped at the camp that evening we all asked Tore about the incident and he is quite scathing about the attitude of some of the snowmobile drivers. He tells us of a similar incident where he found that the driver was drunk so he took the keys out of the ignition and threw them away leaving the driver to find them on his own. One-way of preventing drink driving I suppose.

We set off and start to traverse a mountain face taking us steadily downhill when we get another surprise; appearing over the lip of a ridge in the distance is a lone figure ski touring with a sled. Tore stops and this time is obviously friendlier towards this fellow traveller as we can see him sharing a drink with him. We later learn that he is on a circular tour of the Northern Sweden/Norway area. Totally alone, totally self sufficient, it takes a special breed of individual to take on a challenge like that. We all wave at him as we set off again and he continues his lone trek. Him in his private world and us in each of ours.

We start to descend quite steeply now and find ourselves dropping into a tree line and the forest zone of the lower slopes. It seems strange to refer to it as a forest as the trees look as though they are barely able to survive. In the recent BBC TV Series 'Frozen Planet' David Attenborough explained how at these latitudes the lack of daylight, low temperatures and lack of fluid water sources prevent the trees from growing at the rate that would be normal for their species. They appear to be saplings but in reality are quite old with very slow or little growth.

Suddenly we are dropping quite dramatically and the terrain becomes a real challenge. The track twists and turns through the forest and is tight with large snow banks on each side. The trees mask some of the turns which are really tight. These in turn hide some sudden drops. Very sudden! I negotiate them all safely and start to feel as though I have mastered dog sled driving, as I don't fall at all. I hope that I haven't jinxed myself with these thoughts.

We run for about another half an hour and then comes a very technical manoeuvre. We have to negotiate a sharp left turn over a narrow bridge crossing a small river that is free of ice and flowing quite fast. The bridge is very narrow and has a wooden surface that is snow and ice-free. Tore has elected to tether his team and take control of each of our teams in turn. We dismount and he gets on, executes the turn and stops the sled just as it is lined up on the bridge calling us forward to take over. His only instructions are 'hurry up' and 'don't brake'.

With this obstacle safely negotiated we run through the forest for a while before crossing another river, this time without any assistance, and after a short run we pull off the track to pitch camp. Despite the initial grey start and a few short-lived snow flurries it has been a good day. The running has been a mixture of terrain and we have covered a considerable distance as we have run for longer than any other day. In the late afternoon the clouds cleared and the sun came out. As we stop to pitch camp we have blue skies and a magnificent sunset.

Once we have all secured our sleds and dog teams, Tore calls us together for a review of the day. It turns out that we have put in 60 kilometres today and have made up for some of the lost time and distance, as well as running for the longest period so far. The good news is that he wants an early start in the morning so we can put in another long run.

The area we have stopped in is at the edge of a forest and is relatively flat and spacious. With the river easy walking distance away there is no need to melt snow for cooking and drinking water. I do a check with my handheld GPS device to get our position and turn on my mobile phone, which up to now has not had a signal since we left Tromso and find that we now have one. It is only 2 bars, but we have access to the outside world. I turn everything back off while we get down to tethering the dogs and pitching the tents. The group decides that we will use the Sámi tent, which up to now has been in the bottom of my sled, and gather together for our evening meal.

This will be the first time that we have interacted as a group since the first meal at the centre on the night we arrived. Up to now we have had just our tent team, with one or two others close by, but have not really had any close contact for a prolonged period. Perhaps the main reason being that by the time we had got to grips with the dogs, the tents, cooked, eaten and cleaned up we were all ready for bed.

Everybody has the lines out and the dogs tethered in record time, our 18 animals took us about an hour, which is pretty speedy, and an improvement on the previous few days. They are fed and almost straight away they bed down and go to sleep. The unofficial motto of all uniform services of "eat, drink and sleep when you can, as you never know when it will be denied" seems to be ingrained in these animals. Perhaps they have more to teach us than we care to think.

Tore joins Tony, Rod and I as we unpack the Sámi tent and it transpires that it is new and he has never put it up before. At last! Something that the Norwegian superman cannot do. Much hilarity ensues as we struggle with finding which way up various poles fit, where the guy ropes attach and where the door is. Not an easy task with a tent that is some 3 metres tall and hangs like a limp flag. It reminds me of the Bell Tents that we used to use in the Scouts and I remember the trick of having someone inside holding it vertical and spinning it round to get the door facing the right way and then the other team member pull on the guy ropes to secure it. On completion we agree that the others can take it down as it will probably be windy in the morning and we have no desire to go hang gliding.

A group of us wander down to the river to get drinking water and on the way pass a warning notice on a pole declaring that the area we are in is a rocket firing range. As warnings go it is a bit understated to say the least and we begin to wonder if it is left over from some previous military activity that has now stopped. I later found out that the area in which we were is actually used for the launching of rockets containing weather measuring instruments and other scientific equipment. All I can hope for is that they take more action than just a notice on a pole when they actually start doing it, even if the area is hardly populated.

We collect water from the river and although it is free flowing and obviously fed by snowmelt it is not what I would call the most inviting I have seen. There are bits of plant material floating, and no doubt some small animals, swimming it and although we will be boiling it I personally would prefer to melt snow as that has always produced some of the freshest tasting water I have ever had, especially when it has chilled in my drinking bottle in the front pocket of my sled.

Back at the tent the whole team have gathered and have set up their various cooking pots in a communal kitchen and there is a party atmosphere starting to emerge. I look round for Tony and find him just behind our tent busily digging away in a snowdrift. Intrigued, I wander over to join him and find that he is building a round walled structure that he has designated as a toilet area to afford some degree of privacy. Someone produces a roll of toilet paper in a plastic bag on a stick, which is mounted on the wall. This device is immediately christened as the latest gadget to emerge from Ikea, a waterproof toilet roll holder. The general hilarity is added to when Tony announces that the 'Ig Loo' is ready for use.

As we all gather for the meal I start to feel bit of an outsider again. I suppose that this is understandable. The majority of the group are from Isle of Man and working for the same charity, the three from London are nearer the age of the majority and have more in common in general terms. I have no problems with this and busy myself with keeping my journal up to date and having a quick chat with Pauline while I have a phone signal. She sounds OK and tells me that everything is fine and that she has been busy with various jobs and the like. That is a weight off my mind, as I know that if she had nothing to do then she would have been worrying about me. Interestingly she tells me that one of the members of my Rotary Club has been calling for updates on the trip so he can report to the club members on my progress. It seems he was disappointed to hear that I had not been in touch since arrival and somewhat amazed that the phones hadn't worked. Just goes to show how we have come to accept the ease of modern communications. I don't linger on the call, as I want to save the battery for when we complete the trip and besides which Pauline is about to go out and visit our Daughter, Rebecca, so she doesn't have time for a long chat.

"Hello dear how's the Arctic? Got to go I'm off out for tea. Bye" is about the limit of it all.
Shackleton, Scott et al never had to put up with that. Such is progress.

As it starts to get dark we sit in the Sámi tent and start to swop tales of the last few days and how we are all finding it. Someone has produced another bottle of Port which is being passed round in strict dinner protocol, always to the left with hoots of derision directed at anyone even thinking about sending it the wrong way round. How terribly, terribly British.

We are hoping to see the Northern lights tonight but the cloud cover has returned so it looks like we will be out of luck. I am beginning to wonder if I will ever see them as they appear in the photographs

People start to drift off to their own tents as tomorrow promises to be another long day with some technical challenges as we descend the last part of the mountains and start our runs across the lakes. Rod announces that he is going to sleep in the Sámi tent tonight so that Tony and I can have a bit more room in our tent; at least it gives us a bit more room for the struggle into the sleeping gear, which tonight can be accomplished without kicking a tent buddy.

Thursday 29 March 2012
4th camp to 5th camp N 68° 00'537 E 20° 23'626
Distance covered – 60 Kilometres

Our day starts as usual at 05:30, which allows us to be leisurely about breakfast, breaking down the tent and packing the gear away. Rod emerges from the Sámi

63

tent and declares that it was the most uncomfortable and coldest night he has yet had. It turned out that with so much room he kept rolling off his sleeping mat onto the hard packed snow and getting very, very cold.

We seem to have this breaking camp off to a fine art now; we breakfast, feed the dogs, pack everything away and have time for a brew before we harness the dogs. Tony, Rod and I relent about the Sámi tent and take it down and pack it away, mostly as it finds us something to do other than stand about and wait, but also because as it travels in our sleds we wanted to get everything packed away. This morning the two lads in the end tent are late rising, apparently they slept through the noise everyone else was making, which delays the off by ½ hour, not much but a long time to be standing about in the cold.

The teams set off and almost immediately we are back into narrow trails between the trees and it is soon apparent that this is going to be hard. The trail is narrow, steep, bumpy, and twisty, with overhanging branches and everyone bunches up. This really tests our abilities as sled drivers. We have to strike the balance between making progress without putting too much strain on the dogs due to braking. The real test is keeping ourselves, and the sleds, upright and not getting too close to the team in front.

Even in this terrain there is beauty at every turn as the clouds start to clear and the sun makes an appearance. It is low in the sky and filtering through the trees and the surroundings take on an almost painting like quality that is wonderful to view. The dogs are settled into their running and the only noise is the swish of the runners on the compacted snow, punctuated briefly by the occasional scraping noise as the sled runs over an fallen tree branch, or exposed rock outcrop that has become uncovered on a corner. On straighter sections the slope is downhill and away from us and has been cut up by the passage of snow mobiles, leaving some quite alarming peaks and troughs that have to be negotiated at a fair speed. The dogs are running free at times with the sled travelling under its own momentum. This creates a lot of jerking when the sled hits a peak and slows. This causes the dogs to pull harder against the sudden strain, which is quickly released. It also proves exhilarating, as at times the whole sled is airborne when it shoots off a peak at speed. This requires an effort to keep my balance on the narrow runners as we meet the ground with a resounding thump.

We are almost at the bottom of the slopes when I see Rod start to execute a sharp right turn and drop from view. As I get to the start of the turn I see him bouncing round a left turn about another 15 metres down the hill and become absorbed by his struggle. My concentration is broken as the dogs start to descend without me braking to prevent the sled over running. This has the knock on effect of freeing them from pulling and allows them to increase their pace. This then jerks the sled causing it to shoot forward.

The dogs make the left turn but the sled, and me, are airborne and we don't. I crash into the snow bank and start to fall just as the dogs take the strain and pull the sled. I hang on to the sled, by instinct now, and seem to be falling for an absolute age before crashing to the ground. I am winded and my neck whips to the side with a loud crack. For a few moments I am unsure where I am and hear Rod calling to me that he has my dogs and to lie still to recover as Linus comes to my help. My view about the skill, ability and daring of the long distance sled riders goes up another notch.

When I recover and get back on the sled I see that I had dropped about my own height, 5'10" or 1.6 metres, and that I had narrowly missed a soft snow bank that would have broken my fall. Or perhaps made things worse as who knows what lurks under the snow covering? Had I been able to execute the turn I was only 25 metres from level ground. It just goes to show that loss of concentration can be a painful event in the wrong circumstances.

Shaken, but not put off, I climb back on and set off. As we get going I feel my ribs and neck start to ache and it beings to dawn on me that I am going to be stiff and sore before the end of the day. Still, it is all part of the experience even if it was the first one that I would gladly have missed.

The level ground we have arrived at is the start of the Swedish lakes. Kilometre after kilometre of flat, smooth, hard frozen surface. Well that's what it looks like. In reality the surface is uneven, almost as though the waves on the surface of the lake had been instantly frozen. Even though there is still much to concentrate on; watching the dogs; keeping line to keep tight; steering the sled and watching the route ahead, this is the most relaxing part of the journey so far.

The views are far from empty and boring, for a start the sun is now blazing high in the sky and the clouds have all dissipated. The edges of the lakes are fringed with forests; real forests now, huge trees that tower majestically toward the sky. Every so often there are a group of farm buildings on the shoreline and the occupants wave at us as they go about their daily business. I cannot help but wonder how many days they go without seeing someone pass, especially in the depths of winter. There are also smaller buildings which are obviously holiday cottages as they are shuttered up against the biting cold and driving snow, each with its own boat jetty reaching out into the frozen lake.

Out comes the iPod for the first time since we set off and I listen to Garth Brookes and Pink Floyd as we swish across the lake surface. In a show of bravado (to no one but myself) I even manage to make a cup of coffee while moving, now that shows real sled driving ability! It took about 10 minutes of fumbling and cursing the uneven surface but I was determined to succeed and did.

Taking photographs and operating the video camera on the move was mastered a few days ago so I branch out and use the big video camera to take some footage. The biggest challenge was not dropping it, as it was quite clumsy compared to the small, handlebar mounted version, so it soon went back in the bag.

Once into the routine of the running, I found myself contemplating all manner of things, mostly reflecting on my life so far. I consider myself fortunate in that I am financially secure and want for little in the way of material things; I have a supportive family and some great friends who can be relied on in times of difficulty. My membership of Rotary International has opened up some amazing opportunities and allowed me to witness parts of the world through the eyes of local people rather than as a tourist being herded past on a strict timetable. I am healthy enough to undertake most of the things I want to do and received an education that prepared me for the future and taught me the value of seeking out information and experiences. That's not to say it has all been a bed of roses, far from it as anyone who knows me understands, but I do count myself as lucky to have all these benefits.

One theme that consistently keeps coming back to mind is the environment that I am in. As I have stated before there is little sign of the hand of man in these regions and what there is blends in harmoniously rather than imposing. Perhaps the wilderness regions should be given some form of legal status that will prevent them from becoming developed, mined or in any other way desecrated to preserve them for the future. Not just for man as a traveller and explorer, but for every species on this planet, our joint home.

Once or twice I find myself thinking about the ice we are riding on. Apparently it is a couple of metres thick and strong enough for a truck to drive on, but when I pass through a pool of water standing on a slight indentation of the ice I do wonder.

Surprise, surprise we actually had a stop for lunch today. A proper stop, one that involves putting out the ground anchor, getting off the sled, eating while not moving and then walking about and talking to the others. The dogs show us the proper way to have a lunch break; they promptly lie down, curl up and go to sleep. Tore tells us that we have three more lakes to cover before we get to the campsite and that is still some 30 kilometres away. Now I know the reason for the stop, its to give the dogs a rest not us a leisurely lunch. Did I really expect that he was worried about us?

We mount up again after about a 30-minute stop and are soon back on the trail. The lie of the land is such that this area must be almost entirely lakes with just small strips of land between them, or perhaps it just seems like that because the lakes are so big. I have moved on to Toby Keith on the iPod now and wonder if anyone can hear me singing along to "How Do You Like Me Now?"

Not that I care, just that it probably sounds like a strange question to be shouting in the middle of a frozen lake being pulled along at 10KPH by 6 dogs whilst standing on a sled. I wonder what Mr Keith would think, him being from the Southern States of The USA, a place not exactly known for its abundance of snow.

We arrive at the campsite just as the sun starts to go down. It is still a clear sky and promises to stay that way. The lack of cloud cover has meant that the temperature during the day has been around -6°C at its warmest so the night will drop further. Last night was about -15°C so how much lower will it go? With the cold and clear conditions there is a chance that we may se the Northern Lights, which would really make for a magical show to end our expedition, so we all hope for the best.

Once again we swing into the routine of setting out the tether line and unhitching the dogs. For the last couple of days Tony has had a problem with his dogs, as one of his middle pair is a bitch that has started to come into season. The lead dogs keep vying for the right to mate with her and between the restriction of the harness, the fighting with each other and her fighting them off there has been no success in that department. I have been the lead in putting out the line today and as a result am at the head of the line being passed the dogs to clip on. The first two go on OK and then the third one is the one in season. Tony does not tell me so I clip her on as normal, right next to the other dogs. No sooner have I turned my back to go and meet the Rod with the next dog when the commotion starts. The two leads are fighting for the attention of the lady in question. A swift lump of snow to their heads cures that immediate problem and I call out to Tony to see if we should have a gap or some sort of separation between the dogs. He calls back that he had not been told to do that the previous nights and that he thought the chains would stop them from being successful at mating.

The short answer is, no it didn't, and a mating takes place. It seems that desire will overcome adversity in just about any circumstances. At least it has stopped the fighting and the noise that accompanies it. A little later Tore comes along checking on the dogs and remarks about the incident saying that "This means I will have to kill some puppies this summer". A couple of the girls are nearby overhear this and when we speak to them later they are a bit upset.

One of the advantages of having been posted to a rural station whilst in the Police is that I have had quite a lot of dealings with farmers and in many respects Tore is just like them. With almost 300 dogs at his centre there will always be some that are having a litter of pups and not all of them will be suitable for the job of sled dog, in the same way that farm dogs sometimes turn out to be unsuitable for working sheep. There being no room for a mouth that doesn't earn its feed, measures have to be taken that may not be to the liking of some, but are an everyday fact of life for others.

While posted to Hebden Bridge I visited a farm where such a situation existed in that the farmer had a Border Collie pup that was all white with a black head, a negative image of the standard sheepdog, who he assured me would 'get necked if tha don't tek it; white dogs never work sheep' (This translates to: - "I shall put it down if you don't become the owner" and "At half a mile it will look like a sheep and I will be confused") So, of course, this puppy became Rob, our family pet. I can never be sure if the farmer would have carried out his threat but I gained a faithful companion for the next 9 years until his untimely passing. The funny thing was he was always scared of sheep. That could be because the farmer dropped him into a pen with a ram for a few minutes before we left the farm. A swift, although slightly cruel, way of ensuring it never even tried to worry sheep in the future.

Like most people who have had a dog as a companion, I swore blind that I wouldn't have another. And just like all the others, some 2 years later when I met Bess, a six month old Border Collie who had been returned to the farmer. I shall refrain from going into why and what state she was in. Bess is mentioned in various places in this account and was by my side for 14 very happy years. We had a special bond, the two of us, as she helped me through a dark part of my life and I showed her she could trust someone. But that is another story for another day.

Mind you, I can pick them - Bess was frightened of sheep as well!

The tents this evening are actually quite close together and we can observe each other's groups a little better and some of the camp dynamics are interesting. We have two members who are almost permanently cuddling their dogs like they are some sort of prize toy poodles. To the extent of not bothering about their own shelter and cooking requirements. Some of the younger lads suddenly want to be Bear Grylls, chop a tree down and light a fire. They set about it with gusto, but not much idea. The girls stick together and seem to chat endlessly, as women do. All that is missing is the handbags in the middle.

They are all a good bunch of people but I still consider myself as the outsider. I have worked well with Tony & Rod, and had time to chat amiably with some of the other Isle of Man team. Still I do not feel fully part of the whole gang. Having worked around teams all my adult life and been involved in the teaching of Leadership and Teamwork for the last 16 years I have a philosophical approach and actually take some learning points from the whole thing. One of the major planks of teamwork theory is from Tuckman with his "Form; Storm; Norm; Perform" model. This highlights the development stages when people get together to become a co-operative group. Given that the majority of the time we have acted as individuals, only becoming a 'team' for tasks at the start and end of the day, it would take some considerable time for us as a group to form what would be recognised as a 'Performing' team under Tuckman's model. One thing that occurs to me is that we have not been tested as a group, with a task or situation that required leadership. Should we have been faced with a challenge requiring us to act as a team it would have been interesting to observe.

As the largest group, the Isle of Man contingent are the ones that begin to talk amongst themselves about organising a collection for the guides. They settle on an amount and propose it to everyone, and we all agree. Then comes the surprise; they want me to present it to the guides and make a short speech on behalf of everyone.

I ask why me? Given that there are the largest group and have the biggest contribution, I would have thought it sat better with their group. No, they are insistent that they want me to do it on everyone's behalf. Tony tells me later that they thought that as a Rotarian I would have experience at this sort of thing and would not be fazed by it. Perhaps I had my thoughts on Tuckman a bit wrong and that we were at the norm stage sooner than I thought.

Our tent needs to fill up on fuel for cooking so I wander down to the leaders' little camp. As we are filling the containers up I get talking to Tore about the way of life he leads and how I envy him. In return he asks what led me to want to undertake the challenge. I tell him about Uncle Graham and his stories of living in Alaska and of reading the accounts of the polar explorers over the years. From talking to him it is clear that he simply exists to be out in the wilds, running with dog teams or undertaking climbing expeditions. A lifestyle that I seriously envy but realise that it is too late for me to change careers now.

My advice to the youngsters I work with has always been to do what they want to do; to follow their dreams; to make their own path in life. In many ways I did, with my career in the Police Service, but if I had tasted this life 40 years ago then my path might have been completely different.

Back at the tent we set about cooking the evening meal and generally chatting when Rod suddenly comments that he thinks it must have been hard for me to get on, given that I didn't know anyone before we met and am seriously outnumbered by people who do know each other. I tell him that it hasn't been a problem and truly it hasn't. I like to think I can fit in about anywhere and get along with just about anybody; life is far too short to have it any other way. Equally happy alone or in a crowd is the best way to describe how I feel. But its nice that he considers things like that and I thank him for his thoughts.

As we finish the meal and clean up it has become pitch black and slowly the stars start to come out, shining like diamond pinpricks on a black velvet sheet. The moon is low in the sky and not as big as the night on top of the mountain, so there is a chance of the Northern Lights being seen. A quick check on the guidebook someone has with them and we learn that after 9pm is the time we can best expect them to start. So we make a brew and stand about chatting to each other.

Never in my life have I had a conversation with someone while we both stand with our heads tilted back as far as they will go, staring up into the inky blackness of the northern night sky. When I look round I see that everyone is doing the same. It looks like some sort of strange tribal ritual seen in a National Geographic TV magazine.

This is the first time I have had chance for a conversation of any length with the girls and it seems strange to be back at the beginning stages of conversations (the storm section in Tuckman). Even though we have actually been together for a week we have only had short interactions and conversations.

I learn that one of the girls, who is vegetarian, has been supplied with the same food for all five days, no variety at all. To make things worse it was the fish curry and she is not a lover of fish either. Bad planning on the part of the organisers especially as they have been given advance notice of our dietary needs and an example of how wrong things can go when there is no attention to detail.

We talk about this and that, but eventually the efforts of the day and the rapidly lowering temperatures force us to abandon our quest for the Aurora Borealis and we all head off to bed. I shall always wonder if they made an appearance and then put on a show that lasted for hours once we had all fallen asleep.

Tore has told us that we must be at the finishing point in Kiruna for 10am so that we have enough time to load the vehicles before setting off for the 6 hour journey back to Tromso. It is made all the more urgent as we are 25 Kilometres away, which is a little further than normal, and the drivers run the risk of running out of time for the journey if we are late. He suggests, and we agree that we all get up at 5am and get ready to move off as soon as it is light.

Friday 30th March 2012
5th camp to Kiruna N 67° 50'893 E 20° 33'804
Distance covered – 25 Kilometres

During the night the temperature dropped dramatically as the sky remained clear and a wind started up. I was woken a few times during the night with an icy blast on my face as the wind sneaked into the tent. 5am arrives and as the one facing the door it is my job to get out first. The zip on my sleeping back won't budge and I have to breathe on it, and spit on it to melt some of the ice that has formed before I can get it to move. The inside of the tent has ice on the walls where condensation from our breath has frozen.

I open a flask to make a brew for the lads. What had been hot water when it went into the flasks has now become just above lukewarm. I was once told not to use boiling water to make coffee as it 'bruises' the beans. Not much chance of that this morning. I found out later that it had got down to at least -25°C. I say 'at least' because the gauge didn't go any further. That had been the coldest night of my life and still only gave me a tiny insight to the conditions experienced by the real heroes of my life, the polar explorers.

It is still well below zero as we start to get ourselves organised; we pack away our personal gear and I set to and melt snow for a hot brew and some food while the other two start to take the tent down. There is a small problem with this in that the poles for the tent have frozen into one long line and will not break down into their individual sections. The only solution is to cup it in a hand and breathe on it to melt the ice. There is a hilarious moment when we look up and see one of the girls doing the same, except she has licked the pole and now has it stuck to her tongue. Fortunately she is not injured and laughed as much as we did. Well she did when the pole was off her tongue.

In record time we get all the gear packed away, the dogs harnessed, everything checked and we are ready for off. The first problem of the day arises when I find that my ground anchor has frozen solid in the snow that has become one huge block of ice. I shall know next time to release it and reset it before harnessing the dogs, as no amount of heaving on the line or kicking the anchor will release it. One of the lads comes from behind with a shovel and digs away around it while I stand on the brake to prevent the dogs from setting off. After a few frantic minutes he has managed to release it and I am ready to go.

I travel exactly one metre and fall over as the deep snow under the right runner suddenly gives way under me. Using my well practised technique I recover and set off again only to fall over to the left after another metre as the snow gives way again. It might have been frozen solid under the sled and around the anchor but just off to the side only the top has a deceptive crust.

With nothing more than a wounded ego I recover again and, manage about 5 metres before sinking into another snow hole and falling over again. This time the dogs have got into their stride and I am getting dragged along. Normally the routine is to hang on to the sled to stop the dogs but this time I have to let go as I am being dragged towards a tree, which looks as though it will do me some damage. I just hope that Linus, who was standing just ahead of me, is able to catch the team.

The ignominy of it all, losing my sled on the last morning. As I struggle to get up I find that the snow is almost waist deep but thankfully has kept out of my clothes. The tree turns from enemy to friend as I use it to lever myself up into an upright position and then 'walk' to where Linus has managed to catch my team. I climb aboard and set off as though it was something I had planned all along. How either of us kept a straight face I have no idea.

After about 200 metres of running through the edge of the forest we drop onto a lake again. As I review this area in my mind it strikes me that the strips of land we are crossing are never more than a couple of kilometres wide and tend to be short uphill and short downhill stretches with a sort of plateau that runs through the trees at the top. The lakes themselves are huge and these small strips of land we are traversing stick out like fingers into them. When I looked at a map later I found that it would have been easier to describe the land as a sea with some small islands in it, rather than land with some lakes.

The running is relatively easy, we still have to balance and correct our direction of travel, but the sun is shining, not a cloud to be seen anywhere. If the weather had been like this from the start the running in the mountains would have been easier, but the trade off would have been having low temperatures both day and night. I start to think about how I can best describe the whole event when I am back home and speaking to the various Rotary Clubs, Schools and companies that have supported me.

I soon realise that words and pictures will hardly do justice to the enormous sense of achievement I have acquired. Nor will they convey the elation I feel at having completed one of the hardest things I have ever undertaken.

Even just describing the terrain of this trip will be difficult and I recall something said by the company representative, Mike Hammond, who said, "The topography of this trip will be as follows
City/ mountain / valley / mountain / valley / mountain / lake /lake / lake / lake /river / Town"
The key to this description being that Mountain = Norway and lake = Sweden

All too soon we have traversed our last section of lake and arrive on the outskirts of Kiruna. It is amazing how suddenly the landscape starts to reveal the presence of man. We can see trucks running on roads in the distance and the tops of tall metal chimneys attached to factories that serve the local industry. We face one final technical challenge on this part of the route; crossing a road via a tunnel that has been cut underneath it. On the face of it not as difficult as some of the things we have faced. As we approach the tunnel Tore and the guide team bring us to a halt and approach us one by one. They tell us that some of the dogs are actually scared of the tunnel and will not enter unless they are travelling fast enough not to have time to think.

So we spread ourselves out and start along this last piece of track. All is going well and soon our little gang of three are ready to progress. Tony clears the tunnel and passes from view. I see Rod start to get toward the end and so follow him when suddenly he stops just before exiting. This leaves me with no choice but to stop in the tunnel, as there is no room for me to pull alongside him.

Not a problem in terms of the dogs being scared but a real problem for my ears! As usual when they stop the dogs immediately start to bark and howl at full volume. This cacophony reverberates up, down and round the metal walls of the tunnel. This in turns gets the dogs more excited as they think there are others teams calling to them, so they howl and bark even louder. It was probably only a few minutes but it seemed like hours and soon my head was reeling with the noise. The sled teams behind me have all stopped short of the tunnel entrance so at least I don't have them joining in and making it into a competition to see who can howl the loudest.

We start to move and I clear the tunnel to find that we are running through a municipal park with trails laid out through it. As the trail we are on starts to descend a wooded section I glance behind and find that I cannot see the teams from behind me. I found out later that the team immediately behind me had refused to enter the tunnel and had had to be led in on foot by Linus, the guide. This had caused a considerable gap in the running order.

The came the next problem. The lead teams had come across a group of snowmobile riders coming up a narrow section of the path and they had to stop whilst they pulled to one side and gave way.

It appears that there is some sort of Highway Code that gives dogs precedence over engines – and rightly so.

There were about eight in their party and they had pulled up onto the snow banks to give us clearance. As we passed I either called 'Tak', which is Swedish for 'Thank You', or gave a short wave. Only a couple of them waved or called back, most of the others looked at us with thunder in their eyes.

The miserable buggers thought they owned the trail when in reality we, the dog sled riders are the real kings of the track. As I pass the last one I hear the roar of snowmobile engines as their drivers start to extricate themselves from the snow bank and climb the track. By my reckoning they had got about a hundred metres before I heard the engines die again as they had to pull over for the last few of our party. I Wish I could have seen the looks on their faces at being forced over twice by this most old fashioned, but efficient, method of transport.

I pull out onto a frozen river, which is so wide it could almost qualify as a lake, and can see buildings in the distance, which the lead team are angling towards. In a few short minutes we arrive at them and see that it is the world famous 'Ice Hotel' but perhaps more importantly we can also see the dog truck and the minibus.

And that's it. We have arrived at Kiruna. We have survived four nights in tents; one night in a cabin; three days of constant snow; low, very low and extremely low temperatures; steep drops; sharp climbs; long, energy sapping traverses; bone jarring terrain; twisting forest trails; wide open vistas; long flat lakes; brilliant sunshine. Oh yes, and a never changing view of dogs bums, harness lines and sled covers.

My hands are grimy and full of little cuts from handling the lines; my thumb ends and first two fingers on each hand are sore with handling the clips and metal lines for the dogs and I have a touch of frost nip in them. My beard and hair are matted and full of ice particles and there isn't a part of my body that doesn't ache from the constant physical activity.

And all I can think is "This is bloody fantastic!"

As we stop and put the ground anchor out for the last time I again find a small tear in my eye as I realise what I have achieved. It may not be as heroic as some of the exploits that have been written about, but for a bloke who will soon turn 57 with moderate level of fitness, I think it's a pretty good effort.

Before we have to start loading the truck I have a few minutes for a quick call to home to give Pauline the good news and to tell her that I will ring later for a chat. She sounds a little low and I put this down to it being just before 9am and that I have probably disturbed her morning routine.
It wasn't until I got home two days later that she told me that my dog, Bess, had been ill and she had been up all night with her and was waiting for my friend Peter to come and help take her to the vets for emergency treatment.

It turned out that Bess had developed a brain tumour and about a month after I got home I had to take her for that final journey that saw an end to her suffering. It may seem strange but I am glad that she didn't pass away while I was gone as losing her is bad enough without getting home to find her gone. Fourteen years of shared adventures roaming around the Pennines makes for a very close bond between two souls.

We had one last cuddle and an ear lick from the dogs and then began to load them into the travel kennels, the sleds were emptied and man hauled to the truck for lifting on, the rubbish was collected for disposal and we had one last team gathering.

I made the short speech thanking the guides, not just for giving us an adventure and keeping us safe, but also for helping us raise the funds for our charities, and presented the collection money to them. There were more than a few tears appearing in various eyes when suddenly a loud cry went up from the trucks. We all turned to see one of the younger dogs running up the track with a couple of staff members chasing it. This lightened the mood greatly as we all turned to Tore and reminded him that a bunch of novices had not let a dog get loose, but that a 'professional' handler had.

Obviously the dog would easily outrun the human and was well aware of this as it would run about a hundred metres and then sit down, watching the handlers slipping on the snow and ice. It would get up and set off again when the gap got down to about fifty metres. We were all full of advice, but none of it was practical or heeded. Eventually the dog decided that this was enough fun for one day and after about a kilometre it laid down in the snow. A passing snowmobile driver took hold of it and brought it back. I don't know who looked most sheepish, the dog or the handlers.

Despite the time constraints on us for the journey back to Tromso we were given an hour to visit the Ice Hotel. I declined the offer as I had seen one on a previous visit to Norway and at a cost of £30 to enter was not that keen on seeing another. Most of the others did opt for the visit, some sat and chatted to the Vilmarkssentre staff and I went for a walk into the village cultural centre. Not that I have an interest in these things but because it housed a 'Geocache' which is an interest of mine.

Geocaching is a worldwide sport that uses GPS devices to help locate hidden containers that contain logs for finders to record their visit. If you would like more information on this sport please visit www.geocaching.com. A cross between 'letterboxing', a treasure hunt and a navigation exercise, Geocaching is a great way to go for a walk with a purpose and super fun for kids (of all ages!).

We set off and after a stop for burger and chips in a roadside café we settle in for the long drive back to Tromso. The scenery as we travelled along was stunning and rivalled any we had seen on our trip, in fact at times we could see in the distance mountains that we had been over. Well they were pointed out to us, as from our original viewpoint one mountain slope looked much the same as another. The road journey alone would be one worth taking.

When we get to Tromso we are taken straight to the hotel, which proudly proclaimed that it was the 'SAGA Hotel'. I shall leave the reader to imagine the jokes being directed toward me, as the oldest member of the trip, at this.

Then followed what can only be described as the most surreal moment of the whole trip. As we troop off the bus and into the reception area we are asked to hand over all the gear that was issued to us at the start of the event. The problem is we are wearing it. So the 13 of us start to disrobe from the parka and trousers, untangle the mittens, rummage in bags and find the hats and neck bands and proceed to stand there in our underwear while it is checked off as we hand it over.

All this whilst the receptionist goes about her normal routine of checking people in, giving directions and the hundred and one other jobs she had to do. Not once did she bat an eyelid at these proceedings. More over neither did any of the other guests in the hotel who were passing through.

All I can think is that they are either
A) Broadminded and not in the least worried by people undressing in public
B) Find this normal behaviour at this time of year
C) Wondered what was going on but were too polite to ask
I conclude that it is probably a combination of all three.

Rooms are allocated as we divest ourselves of gear and we are reunited with our bags of 'normal' clothes. Then it's off to the luxury of a shower. As always seems to be my luck I am on the top floor and at the end of a corridor. This means I am unlikely to be disturbed although I doubt that anything will, especially as I have managed to sleep through howling dogs and wild winds over the last week.

On arrival at my room I relish the sheer joy of peeling off the clothes I have been wearing for the last week. Not that they are dirty and smelly but just for the pleasure of being naked. That may seem strange to you my dear reader, but try wearing the same clothes for a week and you will soon see what I mean.

I head for the bathroom and start the shower up to get the room nice and steamy, whilst I indulge my next guilty pleasure, a cup of tea from a real cup not an insulated one. Never did a cup of English breakfast tea taste so good. The simple things in life really are the best.

I clean my teeth, another almost sensual experience, as over the week I have used mouthwash. This is because toothpaste has a tendency to freeze solid and be almost impossible to use. I then head for the bathroom. As I breathe in the steam I feel the inside of my nose tingle with that familiar feeling of needing to blow it and as I do so I realise that I haven't done this action all week. I immediately put it down to the cold clear air and lack of moisture and think nothing more.

Even when I saw a rather alarming lump of something black ejected into the sink, I just put it down to accumulated fluff from the inside of the scarf. I climb into the shower and experienced that wonderful tingle as the hot water cascades over my head and back. I start to run shampoo into my beard.

Suddenly I notice that the walls have blood on them, so does the shower curtain and everything takes on the appearance of something from the Hitchcock film 'Psycho'. Then I realise that my nose is bleeding profusely.

On examination in the mirror I can see that it is my right nostril and surmise that the fluff I saw on blowing my nose was actually a scab and the removal of that had started the bleeding. A plug of toilet paper stops the flow but has to be replaced a few times over the evening before it stops completely. An examination after this showed that I had lost a bit of skin on the inside of my nose and the most likely culprit was ice forming in the nostril. This is confirmed when I get home as an examination of a picture taken soon after setting out on the last morning, when it had been -25ºC during the night, showed that I had a build up of ice in the right nostril. Serves me right for not pulling the scarf up over my nose instead of trying to get some sun to my face.

As I climb back into the shower I get another shock, there is a slug in the tray! Closer examination reveals that I have over reacted. It's the accumulation of fluff from my belly button! Well I had been wearing black merino wool next to my skin for a week, so what could I expect?

I meet my tent buddies in the bar and we have a swift beer before setting out for the meal with the others. We all share an enormous sense of achievement. On arrival at the bar/restaurant that has been recommended, the first thing we see is rows of TV screens showing various winter sports all of which seem to involve Tore and dogs, sleds or skis. Seems he is something of a local celebrity.

As can be expected there was much jollity and retelling of tales. At least one member of the team relaxed so much he fell asleep into his beer! However the story to top them all can only be described as lavatorial humour.

It turns out that one of the big problems for the member that turned back was the lack of proper toilets. On discovering that there was nothing other than the nearest tree for shelter she decided to use the porch area of her tent whilst her buddy stood lookout in the cold. This was probably not the best of places, but the story gets worse. She actually defecated in a Tupperware box, which she promptly sealed up and put in the front of a sled. Not just any sled but the one "buddy" was using.

The unfortunate woman then carried it for three days before getting rid of it at the fishing lake camp. We nearly choked with laughing at that one.

The cost of drinks was astronomical, two thirds of a pint of beer was approximately £8. It didn't stop us sampling a few though. It only seemed fair to liberate a glass as a souvenir, especially as it showed the Artic circle on a map with the brewers' logo.

As we left the bar it was blowing a blizzard and almost as one we declared that this was the coldest we had been throughout the trip. Testimony indeed to the clothing equipment we had been issued with and had used.

Saturday 31st March 2012
Tromso, Norway to Heathrow airport, England

After what seemed like minutes I was awake at my, by now, customary 5-30am. The luxury of another shower, dress, pack and then out for a walk round the town before breakfast. Once again I was able to indulge my interest in Geocaching and managed to get five, one of these representing the northernmost find of my list. I find myself comparing Tromso as a city to Leeds and Bradford near my home. They compare well, apart from the fact that the good burghers of those two fine Yorkshire cities would have a fit at the thought of a metre of snow in the streets at the end of March.

All too soon we are fed and watered and depart for the airport, which, as usual, is full of hurry up and wait. The flights are on time, so no dramas there and if you have seen one airport you have seen them all. Only the currency and language of the newspapers seem to alter, so nothing of interest there either. The journey passes in a haze of boredom, but what can be expected after spending a week like we have. Arrival at Heathrow brings us back to earth with a bump; half finished arrival halls, long queues, and the usual chaos that follows people who have no idea of where they are going, and seem unwilling to ask or read the signs.

The only moment of light relief is when the officer at the passport desk looks at my photo, which has me clean-shaven, and then at me. Resplendently adorned with a set of facial hair that Father Christmas would be proud of, topped with a shock of white hair sprouting at all angles from an otherwise bald head. The look on his face is a picture, as he looks from the photo to me three or four times before I say 'I've just been on an expedition in the arctic'. At this he smiles, shrugs and hands me the passport back. I still wonder what was going through his mind.

We all part with hugs and promises to try and visit, made with the best of intentions but in the knowledge that it will be difficult to achieve. The Isle of Man team have to travel round to Gatwick for their overnight stop. The Londoners have already left as they are on their own doorstep and I pick up the shuttle bus and head for the hotel. Suddenly I am back where I started, all alone at Heathrow Airport.

Only this time I am not filled with any sense of apprehension This time I am someone who has achieved something, set myself a challenging goal and attained it. I have done something that the thousands of others around me wouldn't even consider trying.

That night was a meal for one in a hotel bar, a chance to read a newspaper and the promise of a lie in before the long drive home.

I just wish it could have been done behind a dog sled and team.

The Theodora Children's trust
Appendix i

The Theodora Children's Trust was set up in 1994, when André and Jan Poulie introduced 2 'Giggle Doctors' (entertainers trained to work in the hospital environment) to Great Ormond Street Hospital. When André was a child, he was involved in a serious accident and spent months in hospital. His mother, Théodora, came to visit him every day and it was her optimism and sense of humour that he remembers most from that time, not the pain and worry. In her memory, the Poulie brothers set up the charity to bring the same feeling of happiness to other children in hospital.

In order to reach as many children as possible, since 1994, the number of Giggle Doctors sent into hospital by Theodora Children's Trust has increased considerably. By 2005 there were 7 Giggle Doctors bringing music, magic and laughter to children in hospital through their bedside visits. Since the beginning of 2012, the Theodora Children's Trust has sent 22 Giggle Doctors to improve the lives of children in 18 hospitals across the UK week after week. Today, the Giggle Doctors visit over 60,000 children each year. This year marks the 18th birthday of the charity and also the achievement of having brought laughter to over half a million children.

The profile of the charity has also grown over past years. In 2003, Theodora Children's Trust was awarded the Guardian Charity Award, which honours outstanding charities. In 2007, Glaxo Smith Kline funded an evaluation of the Giggle Doctor programme. Professor Alan Glasper of Southampton University carried out an extensive evaluation and highlighted that the Giggle Doctors fulfil an important role in alleviating the stresses experienced by sick children during hospitalisation. The following year, the work of the charity was again recognised when Theodora Children's Trust was a finalist in the Third Sector Excellence Awards. This year, 2012, the profile of Theodora Children's Trust was raised yet further, when Samantha Cameron, wife of the Prime Minister, David Cameron, hosted a drink reception for the charity at Number 10, Downing Street.

The charity continues to grow and grow. Today, a further 12 Giggle Doctors are being recruited to bring the total number of Giggle Doctors to 34. There is also a long waiting list of hospitals across the UK that are keen for Giggle Doctors to start visiting their sick children.

For more information on The Theodora Children's Trust
Please visit their website: www.theodora.org
You can also contact them by post at:
Theodora Children's Trust, 40 Pentonville Road, London N1 9HF
By telephone: +44 (0) 20 7713 0044 - Fax +44 (0) 20 7713 0066
Or E-mail: theodora.uk@theodora.org
Registered charity no. 1094532

Fund Raising
Appendix ii

The whole aim of the challenge was to raise funds for the Theodora Children's Trust, which was instrumental in me getting the chance to fulfil one of my major aims in life. Like all charities they rely on the generosity of the Great British Public for their donations either directly or through sponsorship of events such as has been described above.

I would like to record my personal thanks to my sponsors as they have assisted me in achieving my aim of raising at least £10,000 to help with the work of the Giggle Doctors as they bring a little happiness to a child's life.

They are: -

Burrwood Accident Repair Centre, Halifax
Handelsbanken, Halifax Branch
Great Kids Toys, Halifax
Briggs Priestly, Halifax
Partline, Bradford
ATEC Electrical Engineers, Halifax
York Sea Scouts
R J Burgess Funeral Directors, Normanton
K7 Services, Halifax
St Mary's Junior School, Halifax

Dignity Funeral Services, Halifax
Stuarts Hardware, Halifax
Niko Distribution, Halifax
Elsie Whitley Innovation centre, Halifax
Keep Safe Self Storage, Halifax
Jack Fielden Joiners, Halifax
Appleyard Lees (patent attorneys), Halifax
Ye Olde Oak (Foods), UK
Rock Inn, Holywell Green, Halifax
Flowquip Ltd, Sowerby Bridge

The Rotary Clubs of: -

Bingley Airedale
Driffield
Malton and Norton
Bridlington
Wakefield

Bradford West
Leeds
Otley Chevin
Northallerton
York Vikings

Halifax	Normanton
Ripon	Sowerby Bridge
Headingly	Huddersfield
Thirsk	Aireborough
Otley	Brighouse
Bradford Bronte	Roundhay
The Inner Wheel Club of Halifax	

I am also grateful for the many personal donations that have been made, especially from the member of Her Majesty's Royal Navy who gave me one days active service pay whilst she was on a tour of duty in Afghanistan. Thank you to each one of you, it made it all worthwhile.

Equipment
Appendix iii

The equipment needed for this expedition falls into two categories that provided by the Vilmarkssentre, Tromso, Norway and my personal kit. The personal kit list was determined following research, advice from the organisers and much valuable assistance from my colleagues at Awesome Adventures in sourcing some items.

Provided by Vilmarkssentre	Provided by self
6 Dogs	Silk socks and gloves
Sled	Merino wool long johns and vest
Tent (to fit three men)	PolarTec long johns and vest
Sámi tent (for group use)	Cotton underpants
Sleeping bag and mats	At night the outerwear was removed and
Cooking stoves and pans	the base layers were covered with: -
Cooking fuel	Sea boot length wool socks
Felt lined cold weather boots	Fleece track suit pants
Quilted bib and brace over trousers	Wool jumper
Quilted Parka	Spare socks (x4), gloves (x2) and
Mittens	thermal underwear (carried but not
Dog food	used)
Food	Thermos flasks (x2)
Frozen 'boil in the bag' meals (mostly reindeer!)	Insulated mug, folding plate, combination fork/knife/spoon
Noodles (dehydrated)	**Food**
Porridge, sliced meats, bread, butter, jam, coffee, powdered milk, chocolate/nut spread, sugar and biscuits	16 Mars Bars, 8 Snickers Bars, 6 Trail Mix Bars, 6 yoghurt bars
Technical Equipment	**Technical Equipment**
Comprehensive First Aid Kit	Handheld JVC video and Sony Alpha

Shovel	stills cameras
Black plastic bin liners	Handlebar mounted sports video camera
	Windproof gas lighter
	Steel and flint 'Swedish fire stick'
	Magellan Explorist Handheld GPS
	iPod & iPhone

Readers should note that the author actually took more clothing than is listed here but as described in the narrative space was at a premium on the sled so most of it was left behind. This gives weight to the maxim of 'packing half as many clothes and twice as much money'

Physiological and Psychological effects
Appendix iv

It would be wrong to say that this trip has not had an effect on me as an individual; an experience that one has waited for almost 50 years is bound to have some impact.

Firstly the physiological effects. Once accepted onto the challenge I made a conscious effort to increase my levels of fitness, specifically stamina and upper body strength, as it was clear to me that walking a dog was not going to be enough. Fortunately the gym program I mentioned in the opening chapter did the trick.

At the start of the training I weighed in at just under 15 stones (95 Kilos) and the program was: -
1Km Static bike ride
4 X 10 repetitions at 20-kilo weight on 4 different machines designed to develop the shoulder and chest area
10 seated leg raises and 10 sit-ups
10 minutes on a treadmill at 5kph
1 Km on a rowing machine
This was completed 3 times per week.

As time went on the regime was increased, mostly in terms of distance and repetitions, and on the day before I left for Norway I weighed in at 13 stone 12 pounds (88 kilos) and felt considerably fitter.

My research into Arctic exploration had given me an insight into the effects that working at constant and/or extreme low temperatures has on the human body. Basically the body burns more calories simply to perform the normal everyday functions. Some accounts have stated that this is in the region of 5,000 calories per day as opposed to the norm of some 1,000 in a temperate climate. If the human 'machine' is required to work harder then this increases.

Although the level of physical activity was not constantly high, there were times when it was, such as harnessing and bedding the dogs and lifting the sled. The entire day was spent standing up absorbing the movement of the sled as it crossed the terrain and therefore keeping the body constantly moving.

Despite the amount, and quantity, of food and chocolate bars, I hesitate to mention the quantity but suffice it to say none of them made it home, I found that I had lost 6 pounds in the week that I was on the challenge and now weighed in at 13st 6 pounds (85.25 Kilos).

It can be seen then that a combination of constantly low, with some extremely low, temperatures and physical activity, loss of body mass is inevitable. Again the maxim for losing weight of 'Eat less, move more" is proved.

Another side effect is that I have continued with my fitness regime on my return and still attend the gym three times a week, work permitting. I actually find that I enjoy the sessions and have increased my fitness levels further as the regime has been increased to: -

7Km Static bike ride in 18 minutes

4 X 20 repetitions at 30 to 45-kilo weights on 4 machines designed to develop the shoulder and chest area

3 X 35 seated leg raises and 3 X 35 sit-ups

5 Km on a rowing machine

The bad news is that my weight remains at 13 Stones 6 pounds and refuses to reduce. Perhaps the gym needs to turn the air conditioning down or I should train in the freezer of the local supermarket.

It is worth noting that although the air temperatures were well below anything I have experienced in everyday life, I never actually felt physically cold at any time. There are all sorts of reasons given, the favourite being that it was a 'dry' cold as opposed to the 'wet' cold we endure in winter in the UK. The primary reason, of course, is the clothing I wore. Wearing several layers of thin clothing is better than one thick layer, as the trapping of air between the layers is an important part of retaining body heat. Additionally the actual materials make a big difference. Silk has tremendous heat retaining properties, even when damp and for this reason was chosen for the base layer for hands and feet. The next layer was Merino wool, which not only retains heat well but also has natural antibacterial properties that reduce the instances of body odour.

The mid layer was a man made fibre, Polar Tec, which is made from recycled plastic bottles. So not only warm but also environmentally friendly. The outer layer, which was provided by the Vilmarkssentre, was specifically designed for use in Arctic conditions and was not only warm but also waterproof. The fur trim on the Parka hood is not there just for decoration. It is designed to catch snow and ice as it blows around the face. Because it is a natural material the snow can be shaken off it easily, something that man made fibres cannot emulate.

The boots were also specifically designed for the purpose with a thick, cleated rubber sole, several layers of material, a waterproof outer shell and a felt inner boot. The mittens were man made fibre with a waterproof cover and were attached to a chest harness to prevent loss. The hat and neck coverings were also of Polar Tec material.

The Psychological effects are a little harder to quantify.

Yes, I have an enormous sense of achievement at what I have done and yes, I am delighted that my efforts have raised a significant sum of money for a very worthy cause.

But there is much more to it than that.

The team dynamics and interactions that I witnessed have given me a greater insight into the theoretical models of teamwork and leadership. That is not to say that I have never had experience of teamwork and leadership, throughout my career in the Police and other charitable activities I have. But I have never had the opportunity of observing them in such a short time frame and potentially dangerous environment with a group of strangers.

I have always been convinced that people have the ability to work together towards a common goal whatever their personal backgrounds, interests and motivations. This is the 'cap badge loyalty' of the armed forces. I now see that they also have the ability to do this with total strangers for a short period of time, with no expectation of a continuing relationship.

In short, people are altruistic and cooperative given the right circumstances.

I have an interest in the impact of human activity on this planet and abhor the waste we create, the damage we do to our home. We are the only species on this planet that has the ability to change the natural architecture without there being a corresponding benefit at some point in the timeline.

This is undoubtedly apparent from some of the comments made in the narrative. The journey I undertook merely touched at the beauty of the Arctic regions and it is my fervent wish that they remained untouched by human hand for the remainder of time.

It would the greatest of tragedies if we did not wake up and realise that this is all we have and we need to look after it.

But, perhaps, the biggest impact has been on my personal outlook on life. I have never shied away from a challenge, opportunity or experience and have seen and done many things in my life that others have not. In this I am grateful to my membership of Rotary International, as through contacts around the world I have done many things. Participating in a Māori challenge ceremony; sleeping in a tin shack in the Australian Outback; standing on top of the Reichstag in Berlin; visiting the execution room and Death Row in an American prison. I cherish these memories and would do them all again in a heartbeat.

However this latest experience has had a deeper effect than the others. I am not sure if it is the aftermath of such an intense experience, or because it is something that has taken a long time to achieve. Perhaps it's the simple fact of having to survive with a small amount of personal gear in a tent. I was, and continue to be, unsettled now I am home.

I find myself questioning why I need all this 'stuff' that I have? Why do we need such a big house? Why do I need so many suits? Life does not need to be complicated or filled with possessions to be enjoyed. I know it is impractical to get rid of everything and just wander off into the sunset, but given half a chance that is my frame of mind. It does not diminish with each passing day

One other side effect is that I now find myself looking for other challenges. I realise that although I am no longer a young man I still have a lot of time left and I want to cram in as much as possible. I want to experience new places and people. If I can raise a few quid for The Theodora Children's trust along the way then that's even better.

Watch this space, as they say.

Printed in Great Britain
by Amazon